My tiny Alaskan oven

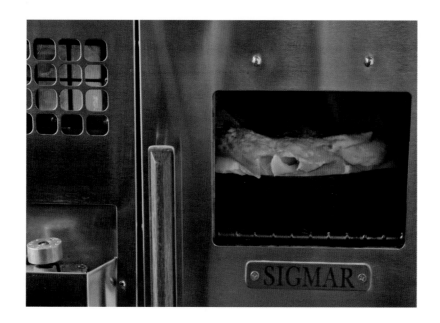

by

LaDonna Gundersen

My
Tiny Alaskan
Oven

Simple Scrumptious

Recipes for Busy People

LaDonna Gundersen

With photographs by Ole Gundersen

Book design and published by Ole and LaDonna Gundersen
Cover design by Ole and LaDonna Gundersen
www.ladonnarose.com

ISBN: 978-1-57833-951-8

File preparation by Vered R. Mares, Todd Communications.

Printed by Everbest Printing Co., Ltd., in Guangzhou, China
through Alaska Print Brokers, Anchorage, Alaska.

LaDonna Rose Publishing
P.O. Box 1200
Ward Cove, Alaska 99928
www.ladonnarose.com
ladonna@ladonnarose.com
www.facebook.com/ladonnarosecooks

Distributied by
Todd Communications
611 E. 12th Ave.
Anchorage, Alaska 99501-1603
Phone: (907) 274-TODD (8633) • Fax: (907) 929-5550
with other offices in Fairbanks, Ketchikan and Juneau, Alaska
sales@toddcom.com • WWW.ALASKABOOKSANDCALENDARS.COM

For Ole,
who made my dream of an Alaskan life
come true. I am so lucky to share the joys
of that life with you.

**The secret to a happy marriage is finding the right person.
You know they're right if you love to be with them all the time.**

– JULIA CHILD

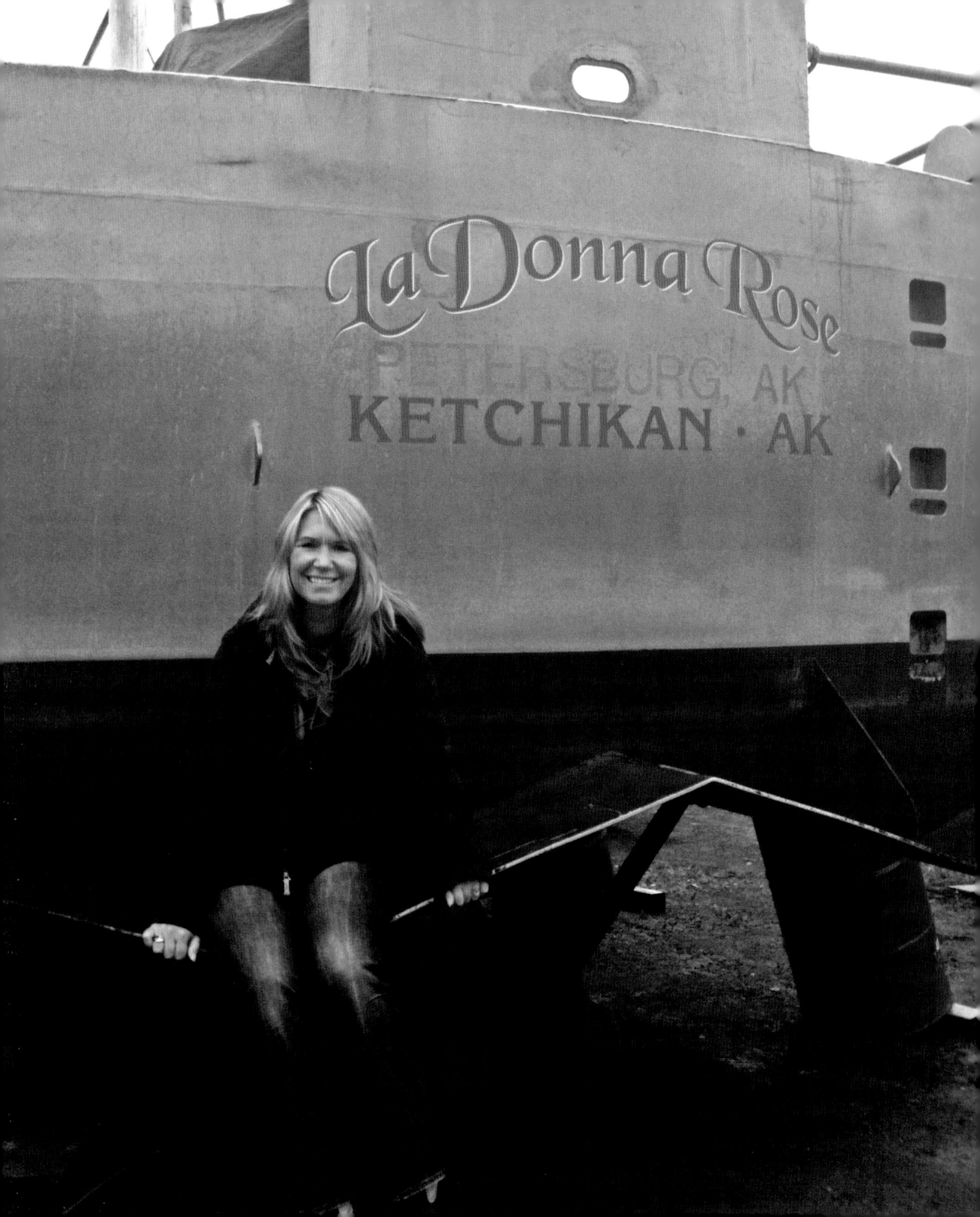
LaDonna Rose
PETERSBURG, AK
KETCHIKAN · AK

CONTENTS

Introduction

I would like to welcome you to my tiny galley kitchen. It would be wonderful if we could all fit in my galley, and if it were possible, I would make each of you a cup of coffee and a rhubarb-lemon muffin. My husband, Ole, who is a commercial salmon fisherman, would humor you with his stories about the biggest fish he has ever caught and the biggest load of salmon he has ever had on board our boat. We would all have a great time swapping fish stories. You should know, however, that although Ole is the fisherman in our family, I am his chief deckhand, galley cook and boat keeper.

How did I get here?

A number of years ago, Ole and I went shopping for a new boat. Ole, who is a Norwegian fisherman at heart, wanted a boat that would "turn on a dime, pack a lot of fish and have comfy bunks down below deck." I am the cook in the family, so I thought it would be nice to have a galley large enough to hold a few people, since I like to entertain and cook. Eventually, we purchased the 32 x 14 foot fishing vessel and named it the *LaDonna Rose*. It was only after the purchase was closed that reality set in. The *LaDonna Rose* did everything Ole wanted it to do, however, the galley was a bit smaller than I would have preferred. I looked at the tiny diesel oil stove in the galley and wondered: "How am I ever going to turn out all of meals we are accustomed to eating with this stove?"

I started out by seeking advise on how to use my tiny stove effectively from other fishermen and was generally told that my stove was strictly used for boiling water for coffee and keeping the cabin warm. One person went so far as to suggest that I should not be in the cabin making home made meals, and should install a microwave oven and eat canned foods so I would have time to be on deck with my husband. Another person told me, cooking takes too much time on a fishing boat and that we should eat candy bars. This is not what I wanted to hear, and since I tend to be on the stubborn side, I decided I was going to master my tiny Alaskan stove and learn to cook wonderful healthy meals with it. My initial goal was to create simple, scrumptious food, that would allow me to tickle my cooking fancy and at the same time make my husband's fisherman's heart go pitter patter. I knew I had my work cut out for me since the top of my tiny Alaskan stove measures 18 x 21-inches, and its tiny "easy bake oven" is only big enough for an 11 x 7-inch pan. Cooking in a small space takes a lot of thought and planning, however, the upside is that it is so small that even when it's dirty, it cleans up very quickly! The great recipes I am sharing with you in this book, are the same recipes I created for and prepare regularly with my tiny Alaskan stove and oven during the fishing season, and cook in our kitchen at home during the winter.

The tale of how a California girl ended up working on a commercial fishing vessel more than two decades ago, and started writing cookbooks is an interesting story. Unfortunately, this interesting story will have to wait for another day and another book.

My culinary skills are self taught and developed "on the job." I did not attend a culinary school or work along side some well known pastry chef to learn to cook fancy meals or pastries. I taught myself how to make wonderful desserts, some so luscious you could gain two pounds just looking at them, while operating a bakery and deli in Poulsbo, Washington. My cooking skills were further honed and expanded during stints at a number of dining establishments in Alaska, including Kay's Kitchen, Annabelle's and Cape Fox Lodge. In addition, I have worked at numerous fisheries inside and outside of Alaska, where I long-lined halibut, red snapper and black cod, gill netted salmon, prawn fished and caught Dungeness crab. Simply put, I am a self taught home and galley cook who loves cooking and working along side my husband. The Alaskan lifestyle is a perfect fit for me, even though it is not worry free, luxurious or comfortable at times.

Ole and I make our living fishing in the summer, and when we are on the boat, I am forced to prepare meals on the fly. Although we love salmon, Ole and I also enjoy good home cooked meals and desserts which forced me to find or create recipes for great meals I could prepare quickly on our oil stove and in our tiny oven. It was a challenge I readily accepted and this was the beginning of many of the recipes you will find in my cookbooks.

There are a million things that get my creative juices flowing. Travel is one of them, along with going to a local restaurant or finding an old recipe rediscovered. I am always on the hunt for a rare culinary find, a recipe that tastes amazing and also doesn't take a long time to put together. The two must-haves of all my recipes are: short ingredient list and, minimal prep time. The two elements place less stress on the cook and make cooking a real joy.

A short ingredient list and minimal prep time put less stress on the cook and make cooking meals more enjoyable.

My recipes are ingredient-driven, which is why certain ingredients make repeat appearances in this book. There are no supermarkets at sea, therefore, I must plan our meals and make the most out of every single ingredient that is available to me. I have literally turned out thousands of seafood and everyday meals over the past couple of decades in our boat's little galley and tiny oil stove by creating and tweaking my various recipes. I have sensitivities to food additives and monosodium glutamate; therefore, all my recipes rely on fresh and minimally processed food.

Roasted Red Pepper,
Bacon and Egg Pastries

Meals prepared using my recipes are flavorful, simple and abundant. These recipes are tried and true, suitable for cooking in small spaces or in grand kitchens with all the greatest appliances, and convenient for busy moms and busy people on the go.

Ole and I live on a commercial fishing boat for five months out of each year and, as the cook in residence, I am required to eat and cook everything from simple weekday breakfasts to big gourmet dinners. Just because I have to cook our meals on or in our tiny oil stove and oven, does not mean you cannot cook these great recipes in your own home. Ole and I don't have a gourmet kitchen, and I have managed to cook up a seafood extravaganza for six, a back deck party for eight or even a romantic four course dinner for two.

Just because I cook in a tiny oil stove and oven, does not mean you need a tiny stove and oven in your kitchen to enjoy these great recipes at your home.

Many of the recipes included in this book can be prepared in 30 minutes or less. They were specifically created to be made with minimal equipment, easy-to-find ingredients and be a breeze to clean up afterwards. The one thing they are not is "boring."

Some of the recipes are ideal for make-ahead meals, like "Sundried Tomato, Basil and Sausage Strata" or "Three-Cheese Mini-Macs." Many are fancy enough to serve to special company like, "Grilled Lamb Chops with Blueberry Rosemary Sauce," "Coconut Shrimp with Green Goddess Dip" or "Halibut in Parchment." I heartily suggest that you make the most of these delicious recipes by using seasonal, organic and non-GMO produce whenever possible. Not only is it better for your health and the environment, but it simply tastes better as well.

I would never claim to have all the answers when it comes to entertaining. There have been many times when I was cooking in our galley kitchen when things went disastrously wrong. One such occasion occurred when I was cooking rice and it stuck to the bottom of the pan. I tried to save it by passing it off as smoked risotto, a recipe which you will note does not appear in this book.

I sincerely hope that *My Tiny Alaskan Oven* will encourage you to cook more often and with more enthusiasm. Finally, I would like to thank you for allowing me to share my cooking world with you and joining us on an exciting Southeast Alaska commercial fishing and cooking adventure and I hope you brought your appetite along for the ride.

LaDonna Rose

Breakfast and Brunch

My favorite meal of the day.

Ketchikan

Is the southernmost city in Alaska, located on the western coast of Revillagigedo Island. With a population of around 14,000, the economy is based on tourism and fishing. Ketchikan is named after Ketchikan Creek, which flows through the town and is also known as the "Salmon Capital in the World," "Rain Capital of Alaska" and "Alaska's First City." The name "Ketchikan" comes from the native term "Katch Kanna," which roughly translates: "Spread Wings of a Thundering Eagle."

Ketchikan's history dates back to 1883, when a man named Snow built a salmon saltery. Two years later, businessmen from Portland, Oregon, hired Mike Martin to investigate possibilities for building a salmon cannery on the banks of Ketchikan Creek. By the early 1900's Martin and the cannery's manager, George Clark, had set up a partnership and opened a saltery and a general store. Two years later the fishing trade flourishing, Ketchikan was definitely in business. Ketchikan became an important trading community, with an estimated two-thirds of the wages reportedly ending up in the bars and bordellos of Creek Street.

Ketchikan has the world's largest collection of standing totem poles, found throughout the city. The Misty Fjords National Monument is one of the area's major attractions.

Currant Scones

The secret to tender scones is to handle the dough as little as possible. The dough may be sticky, but resist the temptation to add more flour, as this will make the scones dry. A sprinkling of sugar before baking gives the scones a sweet, crackling crunch.

MAKES 12 SCONES

2 cups all-purpose flour
¼ cup granulated sugar
1 tablespoon baking powder
⅛ teaspoon sea salt
⅓ cup cold butter, cut into pats
¼ cup currants, raisins or other dried fruit
½ cup heavy cream
1 teaspoon vanilla extract
2 eggs, beaten
course raw sugar or course white sugar, for topping

Preheat your oven to 425 degrees. Line a large baking sheet with parchment paper.

In a large bowl, whisk together the flour, sugar, baking powder and salt until combined. Add the cold butter pieces and using a pastry blender, cut in the butter until the mixture is crumbly. Stir in the currants.

Mix together cream, vanilla and eggs. Take 2 tablespoons out of this mixture and set aside. Add liquid mixture to dry mixture and mix as lightly as possible until just combined.

Gently pat dough into a 12-inch circle and cut it into 12 wedges. Arrange them on the baking sheet, tucking the pointed ends underneath.

Brush the tops with the reserved cream mixture and sprinkle with a little sugar.

Bake the scones for 12 to 15 minutes or until lightly golden. Transfer scones to a rack to cool. Serve warm.

Rhubarb-Lemon Muffins

Good for breakfast or brunch, these quick-to-make muffins are sure to become one of your favorites.

Preheat your oven to 375 degrees. Butter, spray or line 12 muffin cups.

Toss the diced rhubarb in the flour, sugar mixture until coated. Set aside.

In a large bowl, whisk together the 1 cup sugar, milk, oil, eggs and lemon zest until combined.

Using a rubber spatula; fold in the flour, baking powder, salt and ginger. Gently add the rhubarb mixture. Spoon the batter into the prepared muffin tins, filling each cup at least ¾ full. Sprinkle the top of each muffin evenly with the streusel topping mixture and pat it gently onto the batter.

Bake for 20 to 25 minutes or until a toothpick inserted into the center of a muffin comes out clean. Let cool 5 minutes then remove to cool on rack.

Recipe Hint

When shopping for rhubarb, look for firm, crisp unblemished stalks with a bright intense color. Many cooks prefer thinner stalks, as larger ones tend to be overly stringy and tough. Wrap the stalks tightly in plastic and refrigerate them. They should stay crisp for up to five days.

MAKES 12 MUFFINS

FOR THE FLOUR/SUGAR MIXTURE

2 cups fresh rhubarb, ¼-inch dice
2 tablespoons all-purpose flour
2 tablespoons granulated sugar

FOR THE MUFFINS

1 cup granulated sugar
½ cup 2% milk
¼ cup extra-virgin olive oil
2 eggs
1 tablespoon grated lemon zest

2 cups all-purpose flour
1 tablespoon baking powder
½ teaspoon sea salt
½ teaspoon ground ginger

FOR THE STREUSEL TOPPING

½ cup firmly packed light brown sugar
⅓ cup all-purpose flour
⅓ cup old-fashioned rolled oats
¼ cup (½ stick) butter, melted
Combine all with a fork until crumbly.

Chocolate Zucchini Bread

This chocolate zucchini bread is by far the best quick bread I have ever made or tasted. Its texture is soft and moist, its color dark and mysterious. It's perfect and decadent.

Preheat your oven to 350 degrees.

Brush a light coating of melted butter over the insides of two 8 x 4 x 2-inch pans. Dust the insides of each pan with a little flour and tap out the excess.

In a large bowl whisk the flour, baking powder, cinnamon, cocoa powder and salt. Set aside. In a separate large bowl, whisk together the eggs, sugar, oil and vanilla until smoothly blended. Add the zucchini. Switch to a rubber spatula and gently fold the zucchini mixture in the flour mixture; mixing lightly until everything is incorporated. Fold in nuts and the chocolate chips.

Divide the batter evenly among prepared pans, then give each pan a couple of raps against the counter top to settle the batter. Put the pans on a rimmed baking sheet and bake for about 50 to 60 minutes or until a toothpick inserted in the center comes out clean. Cool pans on a wire rack for 10 minutes, turn out of their pans. Invert the bread and cool right side up.

Variations

Bake the bread in mini loaf pans for about 30 minutes. Drizzle melted chocolate over each loaf.

MAKES 2 LOAVES

- 3 cups all-purpose flour
- 1 tablespoon baking powder
- 1 teaspoon ground cinnamon
- 2 teaspoons unsweetened cocoa powder
- 1 teaspoon sea salt
- 2 eggs
- 2 cups granulated sugar
- 1 cup extra-virgin olive oil
- 2 teaspoons vanilla extract
- 2 cups zucchini, coarsely shredded
- 1 cup pecans or walnuts, chopped
- 1 cup dark chocolate chips
- melted butter, for greasing the pans

Yep..."24/7"

As you can see, it is not that glamorous. Long hours, rough weather and then there is the absurdity of having to wear heavy rain gear and boots at the height of the summer heat. It is not enough to be a fisherman. Successful fishermen need to have that undefinable X factor, to make it through an entire season without giving up.

As the days turn into weeks and weeks turn into months... we have a few things throughout our day to look forward to. Simple, scrumptious home cooked meals and 3 o'clock coffee.

What more could a girl ask for...

FOR THE DOUGH

½ cup warm 2% milk (120°F)
¼ teaspoon plus ¼ cup
   granulated sugar
1 package RapidRise yeast (2¼ tsp.)
2 cups all-purpose flour, divided,
   plus additional for dusting
1 large egg
½ teaspoon vanilla extract
½ teaspoon sea salt
5 tablespoons unsalted butter,
   cut into pieces and soft, plus
   additional for bowls and muffin
   tins

FOR THE CHOCOLATE FILLING

1 cup semi-sweet chocolate,
   finely chopped
½ cup granulated sugar
1 teaspoon ground cinnamon
3 tablespoons butter, softened

FOR THE EGG WASH

1 egg
2 teaspoons heavy cream or
   milk

FOR THE STREUSEL TOPPING

2 tablespoons confectioners'
   sugar
2 tablespoons all-purpose flour
2 tablespoons butter, softened
2 tablespoons toasted hazelnuts
   or pecans coarsely chopped

Variation

These can also be made in regular muffin tins, giving you 12. The cooking time will need to be cut back to 15 to 20 minutes.

MAKE THE DOUGH: In a bowl of a stand mixer, sprinkle yeast and ¼ teaspoon sugar over milk and let stand until foamy, about 5 minutes. Add ½ cup flour to yeast mixture and beat at medium speed until combined. Add egg, vanilla, salt and remaining ¼ cup sugar, beat until combined. Reduce speed to low, then mix in remaining 1½ cups flour, ½ cup at a time. Add butter and mix until incorporated, about 5 minutes. Dough will be very sticky and stringy. Butter a large bowl and place dough in it. Cover loosely with plastic wrap and let rise for 45 minutes or until doubled.

MAKE THE FILLING: Place chocolate, ½ cup sugar, cinnamon and 3 tablespoons softened butter in a bowl and stir to combine. Set aside. **Generously butter jumbo muffin pan.**

MAKE THE EGG WASH: Whisk together egg and cream until smooth.

MAKE THE BUNS: Once the dough has doubled, turn it out onto a well floured surface. Roll dough out into an 18" x 12" rectangle with short side nearest you. Sprinkle filling over the dough. Brush some of the egg wash along the shortest edge furthest from you. Starting with the edge nearest you, tightly roll the dough back over the filling, roll the dough into a snug log, pinching firmly along egg washed seam to seal.

MAKE THE STREUSEL TOPPING: Mix all topping ingredients together with a fork.

With a sharp knife gently cut off 2-inch segments and place each in the prepared muffin cup. **Brush the tops with egg wash and sprinkle topping evenly over the top.** Loosely cover pan with buttered plastic wrap and let rise until doubled. Preheat your oven to 350 degrees with rack in the middle. Bake for 20 to 30 minutes. If you have an instant read thermometer, you can check if they are done when it reads 185-190° in the center of each bun. Transfer buns to a rack until cool. Remove from pans and serve.

Chocolate and Cinnamon Babka Buns

I am a huge fan of chocolate babka, which is a sweet, yeast dough rolled and wrapped around a chocolate and cinnamon mixture that when cooked, delightfully melts in your mouth. I first learned about babka from the show Seinfeld and I was intrigued. My second babka experience happened on a trip to New York. Passing by a bakery one day, I was awestruck by the rows and rows of muffins, croissants, danishes and breads, but what stood out above everything else was a chocolate babka bun. I didn't order one, but looking at it I was hooked into the challenge of making my own. I have made this recipe many times and everyone loves it! It's a great recipe and it never fails to bring a smile to all who participate in devouring it.

Croissant French Toast

On family special occasion days, birthdays anniversaries, graduations – start the celebration with breakfast. This stunningly rich chocolate filled french toast; is over the top scrumptious. The chocolate you'll need is available in the candy section of your market.

SERVES 4

With a serrated knife cut the croissants in half lengthwise. Cut a pocket horizontally in each slice of croissant. Cut the candy bar into 6 rectangles. Fill each croissant with a piece of chocolate. In a shallow dish or pie plate, whisk together the eggs, milk, sugar, vanilla and nutmeg. Dip the croissant halves, one at a time, into the egg mixture, turning to coat both sides and being careful not to squeeze out the chocolate filling. Place in a casserole dish for about 15 minutes.

On a griddle or in a large skillet over medium heat, melt 1 tablespoon butter. Cook the slices until golden brown on both sides; serve warm. Garnish with confectioner's sugar, fresh fruit and maple syrup, if desired.

8 small croissants
1 (3-ounce) bar semi-sweet or
    dark chocolate
4 large eggs
¾ cup 2% milk
1 tablespoon granulated sugar
2 teaspoons vanilla extract
⅛ teaspoon ground nutmeg
¼ cup melted butter
¼ cup confectioners' sugar, sifted
fresh fruit
maple syrup

Variation Omit the chocolate.

Sweet-and-Spicy Bacon

It's hard to imagine making bacon even better, but we've done it. As the slices sizzle in the oven, brown sugar and a hint of cayenne and rosemary create an addictive sweet-hot glaze.

4 tablespoons light brown sugar
¼ teaspoon ground cayenne
2 teaspoons fresh rosemary, chopped
¼ teaspoon ground black pepper
1 lb. quality thick-cut bacon (about 16 slices)

Preheat your oven to 350 degrees. Line two rimmed baking sheets with parchment paper; place a wire rack on top of each sheet. Arrange bacon slices in a single layer on the two racks. Evenly sprinkle with brown sugar, cayenne, rosemary and black pepper. Bake until bacon is crisp and browned, rotating sheets halfway through, 30 to 35 minutes. Pat dry with paper towels.

Variation

Use regular package bacon, with shorter cooking times.

Homemade Breakfast Sausage

It's really very easy to make your own breakfast sausage. By making your own at home, you can ensure only the best ingredients are used, plus control the fat content. You may not go back to the store-bought kind.

MAKES 12-14 PATTIES

1 lb. unseasoned ground pork
1 teaspoon grated lemon zest
2 teaspoons paprika
2 teaspoons ground ginger
1 teaspoon fennel seed, crushed
1 teaspoon ground sage
1 teaspoon red pepper flakes, crushed
¼ teaspoon ground nutmeg
¼ teaspoon sea salt
⅛ teaspoon ground black pepper

Mix all ingredients in a large bowl with your hands. Divide the sausage in half and shape into a log; wrap in saran wrap. Twist ends tightly and freeze until slightly firm, about an hour. Slice into ½-inch thick patties and fry over medium heat; browning on both sides. Drain and serve.

Variation

Substitute ground turkey.

Without the Challenge, There is no Adventure

The first time I recall seeing a tiny Alaskan oven, I was on a seine boat out of Ketchikan, Alaska. Ole was a member of the crew on the boat: however, we were not married at that time. I remember looking at the tiny oven with my head tilted to one side and a funny expression on my face. It looked so old fashioned and almost prehistoric and was very dirty, since the five member crew had been working their tails off and had no time to keep it clean. I remember asking one member of the crew: "What is that, and if it was used to heat the galley?" The cook replied: "This is my stove and I cook all of our meals with it." It must have been obvious to the cook that I did not believe him and, if there had been a caption above my head at that time it would had read: "You have to be kidding me?"

The next day we headed out to the salmon fishing grounds and I can clearly remember the sun gingerly setting as we anchored for the night. The chill of the evening filled the wheelhouse and I found myself standing closer and closer to the little stove to stay warm. The crew bunked down below deck alongside the engine compartment and the waves slapping against the stern of the boat quickly lulled me to sleep.

When I awoke a few short hours later, I thought I could smell coffee and a pastry. The smell so overwhelmed me, that I jumped out of bed and climbed up into the galley to see what was taking place. When I got to the galley, there was the cook preparing scrumptious pancakes right on the surface of the stove. Once the pancakes were cooked, he would place them inside the tiny oven to keep them warm. The cook greeted me with a "Good Morning LaDonna, would you like a pancake?" I told him "No thank you, I'll wait for Ole to return with the seine skiff."

I took in all the action the morning had to offer that day, as I watched the fishermen work on deck catching salmon. They worked together in such harmony, laughing, smiling and having great time. I saw Ole pulling alongside the big boat in the seine skiff expecting to get his breakfast. Unfortunately, the cook did not tell me that skiff men are to eat first and since he had not eaten before he left there was no breakfast for him. I felt badly about Ole not getting his breakfast, so I asked if I could make him breakfast while the cook and the rest of the crew were out on deck pulling the next set in. The cook said to me: "Sure, good luck with that." It was such a strange experience since I had absolutely no idea what I was doing. Each time I poured pancake batter onto of the top of stove, the boat would roll and the pancake would spread out into a weird shape. I remember I tried to catch the running batter with a spatula and I ruined a number before I got one right, or so I thought.

The skipper let Ole get out of the seine skiff and come into the galley for breakfast. Ole sat down at the table and I served him the pancakes. He looked down at them and then up at me while the cook laughed. The cook then looked straight at me and said: "Oh I forgot to tell you, Ole likes his pancakes thin!" The pancakes I had made were an inch thick and I had served Ole a stack of four. Ole ate part of one pancake and then praised me for my first attempt with the tiny Alaskan oven. Ole then took his plate of pancakes and jumped back into the seine skiff and headed back out to work. I waved good bye, and when I looked down at the water, I saw three pancakes drifting away from the boat. I learned a great lesson from that experience. Now, whenever I make Ole pancakes, I make them thin and on a cast iron griddle. ✄

Breakfast and Brunch

Apple Pancakes with Orange Butter

Delightful, unexpectedly light pancakes are soft bites of gently cooked apples with the sweet sprinkle of cinnamon sugar and you have a memory-making breakfast indeed!

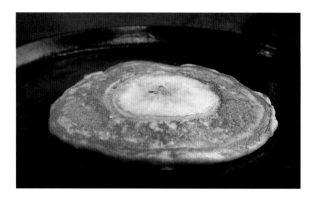

SERVES 4

2 peeled tart apples, 1 cored and finely grated, 1 thinly sliced, seeds removed

2 eggs

2 cups plus 2 tablespoons low-fat buttermilk

4 tablespoons butter, melted

2 teaspoons vanilla extract

2 cups all-purpose flour

⅓ cup granulated sugar, plus 2 tablespoons for sprinkling

2 teaspoons baking powder

1 teaspoon baking soda

1 teaspoon sea salt

½ teaspoon ground nutmeg

FOR THE ORANGE BUTTER

¼ cup (½ stick) butter, softened

½ teaspoon finely grated orange zest

1½ teaspoons orange juice

⅛ teaspoon sea salt

Heat griddle over medium heat, in a large bowl, combine eggs, buttermilk, melted butter and vanilla. Fold in the flour, ⅓ cup sugar, baking powder, baking soda, salt, cinnamon and nutmeg. Stir just until moistened, batter should be slightly lumpy. If too thick add more buttermilk. Gently add the grated apple.

For each pancake, sprinkle ½ teaspoon sugar on 1 apple slice; place onto hot, lightly greased griddle. Pour ⅓ cup batter onto top of apple slice. Turn over when surfaces are bubbly and edges are slightly dry. Cook until pancakes are golden. Serve warm with Orange Butter and maple syrup if desired.

Blueberry Griddle Cakes

Every year Alaskans gather the tiny blueberries, so full of sweet good flavor, often searching out the wild bushes early in the day and tossing a handful into the batter for morning griddle cakes.

In a large bowl, stir together flour, sugar, baking powder and salt.

In a small bowl, combine milk, egg and oil. Add egg mixture all at once to the flour mixture. Stir just until moistened, (batter should be slightly lumpy). Gently fold in the blueberries or sprinkle them onto each pancake as you make them.

Lightly oil a griddle or large skillet; heat over medium heat. For each pancake, spoon a ⅓ cup batter onto the griddle. Cook until several bubbles burst on top and the bottom is golden. Turn over and cook the other side about 2 to 3 minutes, until it is browned.

Serve warm with syrup.

SERVES 4

1¼ cups all-purpose flour
2 tablespoons granulated sugar
2 teaspoons baking powder
¼ teaspoon sea salt
1¼ cups 2% milk
1 large egg
1 tablespoon extra-virgin olive oil
¾ cup blueberries
blueberry syrup or other syrup

Variations Replace the blueberries with one of the following dried fruit options: chopped dried apples, raisins, dates, cranberries, cherries or mixed fruit.

Apple Puffed Pancake

This impressive golden puff of a pancake is baked in a cast iron skillet in a very hot oven. It will fall a little as you carry it, still in the skillet, from oven to table and it should be eaten right away. While it only needs a generous dusting of confectioners' sugar, it is also very good with maple syrup.

Preheat your oven to 425 degrees.

Add the butter to a 10-inch cast iron or oven proof skillet and melt in the oven for about 5 minutes. In a large bowl, whisk together the eggs, milk, flour, sugar, vanilla, salt and cinnamon. Batter will be slightly lumpy. Add the apple slices to the skillet and return to oven until the butter sizzles. Pour batter over the apples and sprinkle with the brown sugar. Bake the pancake 15 to 20 minutes or until puffed and browned. Serve immediately with maple syrup.

Variations

Substitute sliced pears.
Bake in a 9 x 13-inch baking dish.
Dust with confectioners' sugar.

SERVES 4

¼ cup (½ stick) butter
8 eggs
1½ cups 2% milk
1 cup all-purpose flour
3 tablespoons granulated sugar
1 teaspoon vanilla extract
½ teaspoon sea salt
¼ teaspoon ground cinnamon
2 apples, peeled, cored and
   thinly sliced
2 to 3 tablespoons light brown
   sugar
maple syrup

Frittata with Tomato, Zucchini and Caramelized Onions

Frittatas are a great way to both grab produce that's at its peak or as a way to use up a bit of this and that left over from the week's kitchen adventures. This is an easy breakfast to make, making it perfect for lazy weekend mornings and brunches.

SERVES 4

2 tablespoons extra-virgin olive oil
1 small onion, diced
2 garlic cloves, minced
1 medium zucchini, cut into
   ¼-inch thick rounds
6 eggs
½ teaspoon sea salt
¼ teaspoon ground black pepper
1 green onion, minced
¾ cup Colby or Monterey Jack
   cheese
2 to 3 medium tomatoes, cored
   and thinly sliced crosswise

Preheat your oven to 400 degrees.

In a 10-inch nonstick oven proof skillet, warm the oil over medium heat. Add the onions, garlic and zucchini. Cover and cook, until the vegetables are tender. Uncover; cook until the liquid has evaporated.

In a medium bowl, whisk the eggs until frothy. Add the eggs to the pan and swirl to mix with the other ingredients. Season with salt and pepper.

Sprinkle in the green onions and cheese. Starting with the outer edge, arrange tomato slices, slightly overlapping, in a circular pattern on top of egg mixture to cover it entirely. Season to taste with salt and pepper.

Cook until the bottom of the frittata is just set, about 10 minutes, then place the pan in the oven.

Bake until just set and firm to the touch, about 15 minutes. Loosen the edges of the frittata with a spatula and invert onto a plate or cutting board. Cut into wedges and serve immediately.

Variations

Cut into small squares for a vegetable-packed appetizer. Try chopped sautéed mushrooms, bell peppers or anything that sounds good to you. Sprinkle crumbled feta on top.

Crab Cake Eggs Benedict

A traditional brunch entrée, Eggs Benedict is as easy to prepare for eight people as it is for four. It's simply a matter of making the components ahead, then putting them all together to serve. I make these with Salmon Cakes as well and they are equally as delicious.

MAKE THE CRAB CAKES: In a large bowl combine all ingredients, (except sesame seeds and oil) stirring gently to combine. Dividing evenly, form mixture into 8 cakes. Dredge each mound in panko and sesame seeds to coat, set aside.

In a large non-stick skillet over medium-high heat sauté half the cakes in 1½ tablespoons of oil. Cook until golden, about 3 minutes, then carefully flip the cakes over and cook on the other side about 2 minutes more. Transfer to a paper towel-lined plate. Sauté remaining cakes in the same manner.

MAKE THE HOLLANDAISE SAUCE: In a blender, (or whisk by hand) place egg, mustard and lemon juice; whirl at high speed until blended. With blender running, add melted butter a few drops at a time, then increase flow to a steady stream. Season with salt and pepper.

FOR THE POACHED EGGS: Fill a large skillet with enough water to reach a depth of 1½ inches and bring to a boil. Add the vinegar and heat until bubbles form on the pan bottom with an occasional one popping to the top. Break each egg into the water; do not overcrowd. Cook until set to your liking (poke white gently to check for firmness). For soft yolks and firm whites, allow 3 minutes.

TO ASSEMBLE: Place two English muffin halves on each of 4 plates. Divide crab cakes among the muffins and top each with a poached egg and some sauce. Season with pepper.

SERVES 4

FOR THE CRAB CAKES

4 cups fresh Dungeness crabmeat
   (about 4 crab, cooked and cleaned)
½ cup mayonnaise
½ cup fresh parsley, chopped
4 cloves garlic, minced
¼ cup lemon juice
1 large egg
2 teaspoons Dijon mustard
1 tablespoon Old Bay seasoning
1 cup panko bread crumbs, plus ½ to
   ¾ cup for forming

⅛ cup sesame seeds
olive oil or peanut oil for frying

FOR THE HOLLANDAISE SAUCE

1 egg yolk or 1 Tbls. mayonnaise
½ teaspoon Dijon mustard
1½ teaspoons lemon juice
½ cup butter (1 stick) clarified (pg.168)
   or melted
sea salt and black pepper, to taste

8 large eggs
1 teaspoon white vinegar
4 English muffins, split and
   toasted
lemon wedges for serving

Roasted Red Pepper, Bacon and Egg Pastries

Rise and shine! There's no reason to linger in bed when you've got these gorgeous pastries to wake up to.

MAKES 4 PASTRIES

1 **sheet purchased puff pastry, thawed in the refrigerator**
3 **slices good quality bacon, diced**
2 **cloves garlic, minced**
½ **cup onion, finely diced**
¾ **cup red potatoes, diced**
½ **cup purchased roasted red bell peppers, diced**
1 **tablespoon fresh parsley, chopped**
⅛ **teaspoon ground nutmeg**
sea salt and ground black pepper to taste

4 **eggs**
¼ **cup 2% milk**
½ **cup Swiss or Gruyère cheese, grated or cheese on hand**
1 **tablespoon all-purpose flour**
¼ **teaspoon sea salt**
⅛ **teaspoon ground black pepper**
1 **egg, beaten with 1 tablespoon water**
nonstick cooking spray

Preheat your oven to 375 degrees.

Coat four 1-cup oven-proof baking dishes with nonstick cooking spray and place them on a baking sheet and set aside. Crisp the bacon in a large sauté pan over medium-high heat; lift out and drain on a paper towel-lined plate. Leave juices in pan (if you have more than 1 Tbls. pour off some). Add the garlic, onion and potatoes; cover and cook over medium-low heat about 15 minutes or until the potatoes are tender. Stir in the red peppers, reserved bacon, parsley and nutmeg, season with salt and pepper and set aside.

Whisk the eggs, milk, cheese, flour, salt and pepper together in a medium bowl.

Working on a lightly floured work surface, roll out the puff pastry into a 12-inch square. Cut into four equal squares. Carefully fit the pastry into each dish, pressing lightly to get a smooth fit – leave a 1-inch (or slightly more) overhang. Spoon potato mixture equally into each pastry, then pour the egg mixture equally on top. Fold the dough over the filling, brush the top with egg wash and bake for 20 to 25 minutes or until wonderfully puffed, golden and filling is set. Remove from oven and let stand for 5 minutes before unmolding.

Variations

Feel free to double or triple the recipe. These can be made a day ahead and stored covered in the refrigerator. Simply reheat for a few minutes in a 350° oven.

The Ultimate Breakfast Cake

This breakfast cake is showered with apples and brown sugar, it takes on a caramel flavor and develops a sugary syrup that sets it apart from other breakfast cakes. If the urge strikes you and you don't have a 9-inch cast-iron skillet on hand, make the recipe in jumbo muffin cups. The batter is perfect for both and turned out, the cake is impressive.

MAKES ONE 9-INCH CAKE
OR 6 JUMBO MUFFIN CAKES

FOR THE CARAMEL

1 cup firmly packed light brown sugar

¼ cup maple syrup

⅓ cup heavy cream

½ teaspoon sea salt

FOR THE CAKE

1 apple or pear, peeled, cored and thinly sliced

½ pound ground breakfast sausage

1½ cups all-purpose flour

½ cup cornmeal

⅓ cup firmly packed light brown sugar

1 tablespoon baking powder

1 teaspoon baking soda

⅛ teaspoon sea salt

¾ cup low-fat buttermilk

2 tablespoons extra-virgin olive oil

3 eggs

Preheat your oven to 350 degrees. Generously coat a 9-inch cast-iron skillet or oven proof skillet with nonstick cooking spray, set aside.

In a separate small skillet over medium-high heat, brown the sausage. Drain on a paper towel-lined plate. Wipe out skillet.

MAKE THE CARAMEL: **In the same skillet,** add the brown sugar, maple syrup, heavy cream and salt; cook over medium heat, stirring with a wooden spoon, until the sugar melts. Reduce heat to medium-low and simmer for 5 minutes.

MAKE THE CAKE: In a large bowl, whisk together the flour, cornmeal, brown sugar, baking powder, baking soda and salt. **In a separate bowl,** whisk the buttermilk, oil and eggs together and set aside until needed.

Arrange apple slices in the prepared cast-iron skillet. Pour the caramel evenly over the apples. Working with a rubber spatula, stir the sausage into the flour mixture and fold in the buttermilk mixture, mixing only until they are incorporated. Pour the batter evenly over the caramel. Bake the cake for about 30 minutes or until a toothpick inserted in the center comes out clean. Transfer to a rack and cool for 10 minutes, then run a thin knife around the edge of the pan to loosen and unmold the cake. Invert onto a plate.

Serve the cake warm or at room temperature with a generous dollop of lightly whipped cream if desired.

Steak and Egg Breakfast Sandwich

This is a great option for busy mornings. You can use leftover steak or any pre-cooked meat you have on hand from dinner the night before. Tweak the veggies and the cheese to suit your taste too!

Preheat your oven to 350 degrees.

Cut croissants in half horizontally. Place, cut sides up, onto a wire-rack lined baking sheet. Place cheese on bottom halves, dividing evenly. Bake until croissants are warmed through and cheese is melted, 8 to 10 minutes.

Meanwhile, brush flank steak with 1 tablespoon Worcestershire sauce; season with salt and pepper. Let stand 15 minutes at room temperature. In a large nonstick frying pan over medium-high heat, warm 1 tablespoon oil. Add steak and reduce heat to medium; cook, turning once, 3 to 4 minutes per side for medium-rare. Transfer to cutting board; cover loosely with foil. Let rest 5 minutes. Thinly slice the steak across the grain.

In a medium bowl, beat together eggs, salt and pepper. In a medium nonstick fry pan over medium heat, warm 1 tablespoon oil, add eggs; cook stirring occasionally, until curds form, 2-3 minutes. Spoon scrambled eggs onto bottom halves of croissants, dividing evenly. Top with steak, bell peppers, avocado and watercress. Cover each with top half of croissant. Serve at once.

MAKES 6

- 6 croissants
- ½ pound brie cheese (chilled and cut into ¼-inch thick slices)
- 1 flank steak, about ¾ to 1 pound
- sea salt and freshly ground black pepper, to taste
- 1 tablespoon Worcestershire sauce
- 2 tablespoons extra-virgin olive oil
- 8 eggs
- 1 (12-ounce) jar roasted red bell peppers, cut into strips
- 1 avocado, pit removed, thinly sliced
- 6 ounces watercress, arugula or lettuce

Sun-Dried Tomato and Sausage Strata

A golden, puffy strata will elevate the most mundane morning. Layered with buttered cubes of bread and generous quantities of Italian sausage and mozzarella cheese, the dish must be prepared ahead of time, making it ideal for when you have house guests.

Butter a 7 x 11-inch (or 8-inch) baking dish; set aside.

In a skillet over medium-high heat, brown the sausage. Add onions, garlic and mushrooms; cook, stirring until soft. Stir in the sun-dried tomatoes. Remove from heat, let cool 5 minutes.

Butter bread on both sides, stack the bread and cut into small cubes.

In a medium bowl, whisk together eggs, milk, brown sugar, mustard, salt and pepper.

Layer one half of the bread in the prepared pan, one half the sausage mixture, half the cheese and half the basil leaves. Repeat layers. Pour egg mixture over layers. Cover and refrigerate 30 minutes or up to overnight.

Remove strata from refrigerator 30 minutes before baking, (if prepared the night before). Preheat your oven to 350 degrees. Bake (uncovered) until puffed and golden and a toothpick inserted near the center comes out clean, 35 to 40 minutes.

Variations

Substitute cooked ham, bacon or smoked salmon. Feel free to also substitute your favorite bread in this breakfast strata. Whole grain, seedy or country white will be delicious. If you double the recipe, you'll need to increase cooking time to 45 minutes to 1 hour.

SERVES 6

- ½ pound ground Italian sausage
- 1 medium onion, chopped
- 2 garlic cloves, minced
- 1½ cups mushrooms, sliced
- ½ cup sun-dried tomatoes, chopped (if very dry, soak in hot water and drained first)
- 6 slices Italian or French bread (½-inch thick)
- ¼ cup butter, softened, for bread and baking dish
- 6 large eggs
- 1 cup 2% milk
- 1 teaspoon light brown sugar
- 2 teaspoons Dijon mustard
- ¼ teaspoon sea salt
- ¼ teaspoon ground black pepper
- 1½ cups mozzarella cheese, grated
- ½ cup fresh basil leaves, julienned

The pure waters off the largest coastline in the United States provide the perfect rearing grounds for all five species of wild salmon commercially harvested in Alaska. And at the end of their lives, these fish have the uncanny ability to find their way home to the stream of their birth. Alaska owes its abundant salmon runs to good fisheries management and a clean environment. Millions of salmon just keep coming back year after year. And so do the people who depend on the fish to run their small, family fishing operations.

Breakfast Burritos

The next time you want to skip the long lines at the diner, make these flavorful, hearty egg wraps for brunch. Or serve them to the family for a quick weeknight breakfast-for-dinner.

MAKES ONE OMELET

2 eggs
1 tablespoon half-and-half
sea salt and black pepper, to taste
½ tablespoon butter
⅓ cup Monterey Jack cheese
⅓ cup cooked ham, diced
2 tablespoons red bell pepper, diced
2 tablespoons green onions, diced
1 tablespoon jalapeño, diced

FOR THE AVOCADO-TOMATO SALSA

1 avocado, pit removed and diced
2 small tomatoes, seeded and
   diced
2 tablespoons fresh cilantro, chopped
juice of ½ lime
sea salt to taste

Toss together and serve.

In a small bowl whisk the eggs, half-and-half, salt and pepper. Warm tortilla in a preheated skillet; set aside.

Melt butter in a 10-inch nonstick skillet over medium-high heat. Heat until butter bubbles. Pour in egg mixture. With a spatula, pull eggs toward the center from each side. Remove from heat when eggs no longer run but are still quite moist.

Top with filling ingredients, sprinkling them over entire omelet. Slide omelet onto warmed tortilla. To roll, first fold bottom edge of tortilla up 1-inch, then fold sides in 1-inch. Begin rolling, ending seam side down. Let rest for one minute, then cut omelet in half. Serve with avocado-tomato Salsa.

> *Did you know?* Alaska's state flower is the alpine forget-me-not. It was chosen in 1949. The forget-me-not is a perennial that grows 5 to 12 inches high. The flowers have five connected salverform petals, colored sky blue, that are a quarter to a third of an inch wide. They have a white inner ring and a yellow center. The best time to see the forget-me-not is midsummer, from late June to late July.

Sweet Orange Cinnamon Rolls

You don't need to be an expert to tackle the dough used to make this recipe. Sure, yeast dough can be intimidating. But this one is a dynamo, and it is simple to prepare. It's enriched with milk and butter, which guarantees a golden, glossy exterior and decadent, brioche-like texture. These melt-in-your-mouth rolls are worth every minute. Before you know it, everyone will be singing your praises—if their mouths aren't too full!

MAKE THE DOUGH: Heat milk, buttermilk and water in a medium saucepan over medium heat until an instant-read thermometer registers 120°F. Transfer milk to a bowl of a stand mixer fitted with a dough hook. Sprinkle yeast over the milk and let sit until yeast is foamy, about 5 minutes. Stir in the sugar, 3 tablespoons softened butter, 3 cups flour and salt and mix on low speed until dough forms. Increase speed to medium-high; beat for one minute. Add the remaining 2 cups flour. Mix on low speed until dough forms. Increase speed to medium-high; knead until smooth, about 5 minutes. Cover with plastic wrap; let sit until dough doubles in size, about 45 minutes. **Meanwhile,** butter four disposable foil cake pans.

MAKE THE FILLING: Beat softened butter, brown sugar and marmalade in a bowl using a hand mixer until smooth. Add confectioners' and cinnamon; set aside.

MAKE THE ICING: Beat cream cheese, confectioners' sugar, heavy cream and marmalade in a bowl using a hand mixer until smooth. Set aside.

Once the dough has risen, transfer to a well-floured surface **and cut in half.** Roll dough into a 26 x 10-inch rectangle and spread filling evenly over dough, leaving a ½-inch border closest to you. Starting at the end farthest from you, roll the rectangle towards you. Roll it into a tight log, when you reach the end, pinch the seams together and flip the roll so that the seam is face down. Slice into 1½-inch slices. One log will produce 16 rolls. Place 8 rolls in each pan, cut side up, being careful not to over crowd. Repeat the rolling process with the other half of the dough. Cover with plastic wrap or a towel and let rise in a warm place for 45 minutes to 1 hour.

Preheat your oven to 350 degrees. Remove the plastic wrap and bake until golden brown, about 15 to 20 minutes. Cool in pan for 10 to 15 minutes and then drizzle with the icing.

MAKES 32 ROLLS

FOR THE DOUGH

¾ cup 2% milk

½ cup low-fat buttermilk

1 cup water

1 package RapidRise yeast (2¼ tsp.)

¼ cup granulated sugar

3 tablespoons butter, softened,

5 cups all-purpose flour, divided

1½ teaspoons sea salt

FOR THE FILLING

1 cup (2 sticks) butter, softened

¾ cup firmly packed light brown sugar

⅓ cup orange marmalade

2 cups confectioners' sugar

3 tablespoons ground cinnamon

FOR THE ICING

1 (8-ounce package) cream cheese, softened

1½ cups confectioners' sugar

¼ cup heavy cream

2 teaspoons orange marmalade

No stand mixer? Don't worry.
Make the dough by hand.

Pour the heated milk, buttermilk and water into a large bowl, sprinkle yeast over the milk and let sit until yeast is foamy, about 5 minutes. Add the sugar, 3 tablespoons softened butter, 3½ cups of flour and salt. Using a wooden spoon mix until combined, about 1 minute. Add the remaining 1½ cups flour. Mix until dough begins to pull away from sides of bowl. Turn dough out onto a lightly floured work surface and fold it over a few times to incorporate the flour–don't get carried away with it. The dough will be wet and soft. Put it back into the bowl and cover it with plastic wrap or a towel and let rise in a warm place for 1 hour or until doubled.

Variations Roll dough into an 18 x 14-inch rectangle and spread filling evenly over dough leaving a ½-inch border closest to you. Roll up and slice into 12 rolls. Place cut side up in a buttered 9 x 13-inch baking dish. Bake until golden brown, about 25 minutes.

Cutting the rolls into pieces Unflavored dental floss slices cleanly though soft dough. Slide the floss under the dough, cross the strands and pull.

While you are waiting for the dough to rise, make a luscious smoothie!

Pomegranate

In a blender, combine **1 (6-ounce) container berry yogurt, 1 cup frozen mixed berries, 1 cup pomegranate juice, 1-2 teaspoons honey** and **2-3 ice cubes.** Purée until smooth. Serves 2

Strawberry-Kiwi

In a blender, combine **1¼ cups cold apple juice, 1 banana, 1 kiwi fruit, peeled and sliced, 5 frozen strawberries** and **1-2 teaspoons honey.** Purée until smooth. Serves 2

Strawberry

In a blender, combine **1 ripe banana, 2 cups frozen strawberries, 1 cup rice milk** and **1-2 tablespoons honey.** Purée until smooth. Serves 2

Pineapple-Banana

In a blender, combine **1 cup crushed pineapple in juice, 1 banana, 1 (6-ounce) container strawberry/banana yogurt** and **½ cup ice cubes.** Purée until smooth. Sprinkle with **grated nutmeg** and serve. Serves 2

Pumpkin Doughnuts

When the morning air turns crisp and cool, make up some of our favorite doughnuts, lightly spiced with cinnamon and nutmeg. Since these doughnuts are not raised with yeast, preparation time is short. We suggest tossing half the doughnuts (and their "holes") in a mixture of cinnamon and sugar. Not only does this give everyone a choice, it looks pretty, too.

MAKES ABOUT 18 DOUGHNUTS AND HOLES.

FOR THE DOUGHNUTS

2 eggs
1 cup canned pumpkin purée
¾ cup granulated sugar
¼ cup lightly packed brown sugar
½ cup low-fat buttermilk
3 tablespoons butter, melted
4 teaspoons baking powder
½ teaspoon baking soda
1 teaspoon ground cinnamon
½ teaspoon ground nutmeg
1 teaspoon sea salt
3 cups all-purpose flour, plus more for rolling
vegetable oil, (about 4 cups) for frying

FOR THE GLAZE

3½ cups confectioners' sugar
⅓ cup heavy cream
1 tablespoon light corn syrup
½ teaspoon vanilla extract
½ teaspoon ground cardamom
¼ teaspoon sea salt
2-3 tablespoons hot water

MAKE THE DOUGHNUTS: In a large bowl, combine the eggs, pumpkin, sugar, brown sugar, buttermilk and melted butter, stir well to combine. Stir in baking powder, soda, cinnamon, nutmeg and salt.

Sprinkle the flour a little at a time over the pumpkin mixture and stir gently to just combine. Dough will be moist. Turn it out onto a well floured surface and roll it out to about ½-inch thick.

Use a doughnut cutter (or 3-inch and 1-inch biscuit cutters) to cut out the doughnuts. Transfer the doughnuts and holes to a lightly floured baking sheet lined with parchment paper.

Heat 2-inches of oil in 3-quart straight-sided heavy-bottomed pan, over medium heat, until it reaches 350° degrees on a deep-fat thermometer. Carefully drop the doughnuts, a few at a time, into the oil. (They should immediately float to the top and fluff up). Using a metal slotted spatula carefully flip them over. Remove them from the oil as soon as they're golden brown, about 2-3 minutes total. Place the doughnuts on paper-towel lined plates to drain.

MAKE THE GLAZE: In a medium bowl, mix all glaze ingredients until smooth. **First dip:** while the doughnuts are still warm, dip them in the glaze to coat the tops and place them on a rack. **Second dip:** when the first coat of glaze is slightly hardened, dip the doughnut a second time and let glaze set again, if you can wait that long!

Recipe hint For most people, deep frying at home is intimidating. A rocking and rolling boat can also have its own challenges and I only make these when at home, tied up to a dock or at anchor to avoid the risk of getting burned. I drew some conclusions that will prove helpful if you deep-fry them the same way I do:

• Fill the pot no more then one-third full with oil.
• Be patient. Heat the oil slowly over moderate heat for better control.
• Above all, do not move the pot of hot oil around.
• Fry in small batches to help the oil maintain a steady temperature.
• Save the empty oil bottles and strain the oil back into them when it has cooled.

Soup and Salads

*A comforting bowl of warmth or a healthy hearty salad
is often just the thing to make you feel at home.*

Wrangell

Several now famous people made their way through Wrangell in the past, including Wyatt Earp who served as a temporary marshall for 10 days while he and his wife, Josie, were on their way to the Klondike. John Muir wrote of his adventures in Wrangell and Soapy Smith, famed outlaw, used to hide out in Wrangell when things were too hot for him in Skagway.

Wrangell is the third oldest community in Southeast and the only city in Alaska to be ruled by four nations under three flags...Tlingit, Russia, England and the United States.

Wrangell served as the trade center for all of the gold rushes, offering access to the Klondike fields through the Stikine River corridor and then on into the Interior to the Yukon River.

Not long after the purchase of Alaska, the fishing industry got its start with the establishment of several canneries throughout Southeast. The canneries were responsible for the eventual development of the large fish traps at stream mouths that dramatically impacted salmon runs. These traps were later outlawed, but had serious impacts to the local economies, particularly the Tlingit groups who had traditionally procured their subsistence resources from these streams. The Wrangell Museum and Library, have extensive photo collections and other resources on their unique history.

Root Vegetable and Barley Soup

You can never have enough warming soups in your repertoire. No bacon? Add some cooked sliced sausage. Either way, this is a satisfying and comforting way to reward yourself at the end of a chilly day.

SERVES 6

5 slices, quality thick-cut bacon, cut into ½-inch strips
1 medium onion, diced
2 garlic cloves, minced
1 cup pearl barley, picked over, rinsed and drained
8 cups reduced-sodium organic chicken or vegetable broth
1 medium carrot, peeled, diced
1 stalk celery, diced
1 leek, washed, sliced
1 medium turnip, peeled and cut into ½-inch dice
1 medium Yukon Gold potato, peeled and cut into ½-inch dice
1 cup water
2 teaspoons lemon juice
¼ teaspoon ground nutmeg
¼ teaspoon sea salt
¼ teaspoon freshly ground black pepper
⅓ cup fresh parsley, minced

In a heavy soup pot over medium heat, cook the bacon until crisp. Transfer to a paper-towel lined plate, set aside. Add the onions to the bacon fat and cook until soft (should you have more than 1 Tbls. drain off extra). Stir in the garlic and barley, stirring constantly until fragrant. Add the broth, carrots, celery, leeks, turnips, potatoes and 1 cup water. Bring to a simmer and cook covered, stirring occasionally, until the barley and vegetables are tender, about 35 minutes. Add the lemon juice and season with nutmeg, salt and pepper.

Divide the warm soup among bowls. Garnish with the crumbled bacon and a sprinkle of parsley. Serve immediately.

Split Pea Soup with Kielbasa

This soup is probably my most requested meal – it is near perfect. There are a couple of secrets that make this soup so amazing, garlic and basil. This is not your typical boring split pea soup, it's the best split pea soup you will ever eat.

In a heavy soup pot over medium heat, melt the butter. Add the garlic, onion and celery and cook, until the onion is translucent and the celery begins to soften. Stir in the peas and 6 cups water. Bring to a simmer and cook covered, for 25 minutes.

Stir in kielbasa, carrots, potatoes, basil, thyme, mustard, salt and pepper and remaining 2 cups of water. Reduce heat; cover and simmer for 35 to 45 minutes or until peas and vegetables are tender.

Divide the warm soup among bowls. Serve immediately.

SERVES 6

- 3 tablespoons butter
- 4 garlic cloves, minced
- 1 medium onion, diced
- 2 stalks celery, diced
- 1 cup dried green split peas
- 8 cups water, divided
- ½ pound turkey kielbasa, halved lengthwise and sliced
- 3 medium carrots, peeled, thinly sliced
- 2 medium Yukon Gold potatoes (4 cups) peeled and cut into ½-inch dice
- 1 teaspoon dried basil
- ½ teaspoon dried thyme
- 1½ teaspoons ground mustard
- 1 teaspoon sea salt or as needed
- ½ teaspoon ground black pepper, or as needed
- 1 teaspoon dried parsley

Recipe hint

You can substitute fresh herbs for dried herbs at a ratio of one tablespoon fresh to one teaspoon dried.

Italian Wedding Soup

The name "Italian Wedding Soup" is a reference to the marriage of greens and meat in the soup. A favorite in our house and is truly bliss in a bowl.

SERVES 4

FOR THE MEATBALLS

½ pound ground chicken, turkey, pork or Italian sausage

¼ cup Parmesan cheese, grated

3 tablespoons onion, finely diced

2 tablespoons panko bread crumbs

1 tablespoon dried parsley

1 egg, beaten

3 cloves garlic, minced

¼ teaspoon sea salt

freshly ground black pepper

1 teaspoon extra-virgin olive oil

FOR THE SOUP

2 teaspoons extra-virgin olive oil

1 medium onion, chopped

1 medium carrot, peeled, diced

¾ cup orzo pasta or other small pasta

1 medium zucchini, diced

2 cups kale, chopped

8 cups reduced-sodium organic chicken or vegetable broth

½ cup fresh basil, chopped

sea salt and freshly ground black pepper to taste

Parmesan cheese, for garnish

MAKE THE MEATBALLS: Make the meatballs by mixing their ingredients together except the olive oil. Shape mixture into 1-inch meatballs. Heat the 1 teaspoon of olive oil in a heavy soup pot. Brown the meatballs, remove and set aside. Pour off any extra fat in the pan.

MAKE THE SOUP: In the same pan, heat 2 teaspoons olive oil. Add the onion and carrot and cook until softened, scraping up any browned bits off the bottom of the pan when stirring. Stir in the pasta and cook for 1 minute. Stir in zucchini and kale. Add the broth and bring to a boil. Reduce heat, stir in the meatballs and basil simmer gently for 10 minutes. Adjust the consistency of the soup to your preference by adding water or more broth. Season to taste with salt and black pepper.

Divide the warm soup among bowls and serve with grated Parmesan cheese.

Chicken, Corn and Edamame Chowder

To turn this hearty soup into a weeknight feast, serve it with some crusty garlic bread and a mixed green salad. The result is a staggering meal that takes minutes to make.

In a heavy soup pot over medium heat, cook the bacon until crisp. Transfer to a paper-towel lined plate, set aside. Add the onions to the bacon fat and cook, stirring occasionally until soft. Add the broth, potatoes and Italian seasoning. Bring to a simmer and cook, stirring occasionally, until potatoes are tender. Stir in the edamame, creamed corn, chicken, half-and-half and reserved bacon; season with salt and pepper. Stir in the fresh basil. Simmer until edamame are tender.

Divide the warm soup among bowls and serve.

SERVES 4

- 4 slices quality thick-cut bacon, cut into ½-inch strips
- 1 medium onion, diced
- 8 cups reduced-sodium organic chicken or vegetable broth
- 2 red potatoes (2 cups) peeled and cut into ½-inch dice
- ¾ teaspoon dried Italian seasoning
- 2 cups frozen shelled edamame
- 1 (15-ounce) can creamed corn
- 2 cups (cooked) shredded rotisserie chicken or canned chicken (undrained)
- 1½ cups half-and-half
- ⅛ teaspoon sea salt
- ⅛ teaspoon freshly ground black pepper
- ½ cup fresh basil, chopped

What are Edamame? Japanese for "beans on a branch" – are a type of soybean that's picked when young, plump and tender (as opposed to field soybeans, which are harvested when mature and dry). Edamame have a sweet, nutty flavor. Think of them as an alternative to fava beans or lima beans.

Asparagus or Broccoli Cream Soup

These maybe the two of the most flavorful soups you'll eat. Before making the base, you have a choice to make–asparagus or broccoli soup? The stems of whichever you opt for, are used in the base and will be the dominant flavor in the soup. The asparagus tips or broccoli florets will be steamed, then added to the soup just before serving.

SERVES 4

1 lb. asparagus, trim off woody portion and discard. Chop center portion and use in soup base. Steam tips for 3 minutes.

OR...

1 head broccoli, remove florets from stem, trim tough outer layer of stems with a peeler. Chop and use in soup base Cut florets into bite sized pieces and steam for 4 minutes.

4 cups reduced-sodium organic chicken or vegetable broth

2 cups leeks, trimmed, rinsed and chopped (white and light green parts) or 1 lg. onion

1½ cups red potatoes, peeled, cubed

½ cup celery, chopped

1 cup packed fresh parsley, chopped

5 tablespoons butter

¼ cup all purpose flour

3 cups half-and-half

2 tablespoons sherry cooking wine

1 tablespoon lemon juice

sea salt and black pepper, to taste

ground cayenne, optional, to taste

Cook stems and remaining vegetables, broth and parsley in a heavy soup pot over high heat. Bring to a boil, reduce heat and simmer until vegetables are tender, 15 minutes. Purée base in a blender until smooth. Strain and set aside.

Melt butter in the soup pot over medium-low heat. Whisk in flour and cook 1 minute, stirring constantly. Slowly stir in half-and half. Simmer 4-5 minutes over medium heat, stirring constantly until thickened. Add strained soup base, wine and lemon juice. Season with salt and white pepper, to taste. Just before serving add the reserved steamed asparagus tips or broccoli florets.

Parmesan Croutons

2 cups French bread, cut into ¼-inch cubes Toast in 400° oven for 10 minutes.

Melt in sauté pan:

2 tablespoons butter

Add:

½ teaspoon paprika

⅛ teaspoon sea salt

Toasted bread cubes

Toss bread cubes with:

½ cup Parmesan cheese, grated

Chive-Butter Crostini

8 slices baguette-type bread, ½-inch thick. Toast in 400° oven for 10 minutes.

Combine:

¼ cup butter, softened

2 tablespoons fresh chives, chopped

1 tablespoon lemon zest, minced

⅛ teaspoon sea salt

Spread mixture on toasted bread.

Mulligatawny Soup

This soup is fairly spicy, but that's a good thing. It'll actually cool you down. For a tamer dish, use less cayenne, back off on the jalapeño or use a mild curry powder. Heat levels vary with different brands—you may have to experiment. But don't eliminate the heat altogether. Coconut milk helps buffer spiciness, as do the rice, cilantro and Mango-Apple Salad.

Combine mango, apple and lime juice for the salsa; set aside.

In a heavy soup pot over medium-high heat, cook the chicken about 5 minutes. Add the onion, curry, garlic, ginger, jalapeño and cayenne; cook until onion is soft, 4-5 minutes. Stir in broth, tomatoes and cilantro. Bring to a boil, reduce heat and simmer 10 minutes.

Melt butter in a medium saucepan, then whisk in flour. Add about 2 cups strained soup broth and whisk to combine (return solids back to the soup pot). Simmer flour mixture for 1 minute, then stir into soup. Cook soup 2 minutes to thicken. Add the coconut milk. Serve soup over jasmine rice, garnish with Mango-Apple Salad and toasted coconut.

SERVES 4-6

Serve and Garnish with:
Hot "cooked" jasmine rice
Toasted coconut

FOR THE MANGO-APPLE SALSA

1 mango, peeled, diced
1 Granny Smith apple, diced
juice of 1 lime

FOR THE SOUP

1 lb. boneless, skinless chicken thighs, cut into 2-inch pieces, seasoned with sea salt and ground black pepper
1 tablespoon olive oil

1 cup onion, sliced
3 tablespoons curry powder
2 tablespoons garlic, minced
2 tablespoons fresh ginger, minced
1 small jalapeño, seeded, minced
¼ teaspoon ground cayenne, optional

4 cups reduced-sodium organic chicken broth
1 cup tomatoes, seeded, diced
¼ cup fresh cilantro, chopped

2 tablespoons butter
2 tablespoons all-purpose flour
2 cups strained soup broth

1 can coconut milk

Dungeness Crab and Corn Chowder

I am a year-round lover of soup, even on the hottest of summer days. Crab and corn is one of my favorite combinations, complementing each other, creating layer upon layer of savory flavors.

SERVES 4

3 tablespoons butter
1 medium onion, chopped
1 stalk celery, chopped
1 medium carrot, grated
3 cloves garlic, minced
3 cups Yukon Gold potatoes, peeled
   and cut into ½-inch dice
4 cups reduced-sodium organic
   chicken broth
¼ teaspoon sea salt, or as needed
¼ teaspoon freshly ground black
   pepper or as needed
½ teaspoon Old Bay seasoning
2 cups fresh Dungeness crab meat
   (about 2 crab, cooked and cleaned)
2½ cups half-and-half
1 (15-ounce) can creamed corn
1 tablespoon fresh parsley, minced

In a soup pot melt the butter over medium heat. Add the onion, celery, carrot and garlic. Sauté until soft.

Stir in the potatoes, broth, salt, pepper and seasoning. Cover and simmer 20 minutes or until the potatoes are cooked through.

Reduce heat to low and add the crab, half-and-half, creamed corn and parsley, simmer gently until hot.

Ladle the chowder into warm soup bowls and serve immediately.

Skillet Cornbread

SERVES 4-6

1¼ cups yellow cornmeal
1¼ cups all-purpose flour
2 tablespoons sugar
1½ teaspoons baking powder
½ teaspoon baking soda
1¼ teaspoons sea salt
1 large egg
1¾ cups low-fat buttermilk
4 tablespoons butter

Preheat your oven to 425 degrees. Whisk together cornmeal, flour, sugar, baking powder, baking soda and salt in a large bowl; set aside. Whisk together the egg and buttermilk and stir it into the flour mixture.

Melt butter in a 10-inch cast-iron or oven proof skillet in oven. Remove skillet; swirl butter to coat. Pour in batter. Bake 20 to 25 minutes or until a toothpick comes out clean. Cut into wedges.

In the spring of 2013 Ketchikan broke the Guinness World Record for the most participants in a "Rain Boot Race."

me

1,976 people showed up for the race

Queen Shauna and her King

Apple and Spinach Salad

If you have ever experienced the heat of being on a commercial fishing boat in the summer, then you know cooking is not the first thing on anyone's mind in June and July. That is when I go into my "no cook" mode, which offers great inspiration for looking at ingredients, especially seasonal produce in a new light.

SERVES 4

FOR THE VINAIGRETTE

2 tablespoons orange juice
2 tablespoons lime juice
2 teaspoons Dijon mustard
2 teaspoons honey
2 teaspoons shallot, minced
¼ teaspoon sea salt
⅛ teaspoon freshly ground black
   pepper

8 ½-inch baguette slices
1 tablespoon olive oil

FOR THE CARAMELIZED WALNUTS

1 cup walnut halves
1 tablespoon extra-virgin olive oil
½ teaspoon sea salt
2-3 teaspoons granulated sugar
pinch freshly ground black
   pepper
pinch ground cinnamon

FOR THE SALAD

½ cup red onion, thinly sliced
8 cups baby spinach (washed) or
   spring salad greens
2 crisp apples, cored and thinly
   sliced
¼ cup dried cranberries
¼ cup crumbled blue cheese

Preheat your oven to 350 degrees.

MAKE THE VINAIGRETTE: Whisk together all vinaigrette ingredients. Set aside.

Lightly brush the baguette slices with the olive oil. Place in the oven and toast until golden and crisp, 3 to 5 minutes.

MAKE THE CARAMELIZED WALNUTS: Toss walnut halves with all ingredients to coat. Place on a baking sheet in an even layer and roast until lightly toasted, about 10 minutes. Remove from oven and let cool.

MAKE THE SALAD: Just before serving, place the onion, spinach and apple in a large bowl. Drizzle with the vinaigrette, tossing lightly to coat. Place about 2 cups of greens on each plate and sprinkle the cranberries, blue cheese and walnuts on each salad.

Nestle two baguette slices onto each plate and serve.

Honey Mustard Coleslaw

Both of these salads are just right for busy hot summer days and they are perfect to take to a potluck.

Combine cabbage, almonds, cranberries, celery, green onions and green pepper in a large bowl.

Combine all the dressing ingredients, adding salt and pepper to taste. Pour dressing over slaw just before serving. Stir well.

Two Bean Rice Salad

SERVES 4-6

3 cups "cooked" Jasmine rice, chilled
1 (15-ounce) can Pinto beans, rinsed and drained
1 (15-ounce) can Black beans, rinsed and drained
1 (10-ounce) package frozen peas
1 cup celery, sliced
½ cup red onion, chopped
1 (4-ounce) can diced green chili peppers, drained
⅔ cup bottled Paul Newman's original salad dressing

In a large bowl; combine all ingredients. Toss lightly to coat. Season with salt and black pepper, if desired.

SERVES 4-6

1 (16-ounce) bag ready to eat coleslaw
½ cup sliced almonds
1½ cups dried cranberries
½ cup celery, diced
¼ cup green onions
½ cup green bell pepper, chopped

FOR THE DRESSING

½ cup mayonnaise
1 tablespoon sweet pickle relish
1 tablespoon Dijon mustard
2 tablespoons honey
⅛ teaspoon sea salt
freshly ground black pepper, to taste

Seared Scallops with Teriyaki Salad

You just got home and you want a healthier answer to lunch or dinner than prepared foods or take out, but what to make? Here is a quick, fresh and flavorful dish using healthy and delicious ingredients to add to your repertoire.

MAKE THE SAUCE: In a small bowl, combine all sauce ingredients. Reserve half the mixture for the salad, pour the rest over the scallops in a Ziploc plastic bag and put in refrigerator for 20 minutes.

Blanch broccoli and peas in boiling salted water for 1 minute, then drain. Toss with remaining salad ingredients and reserved dressing.

MAKE THE SCALLOPS: Remove the scallops from the marinade, pat dry with paper towels. Heat a 10-inch nonstick skillet over medium-high heat. Add the oil and heat until hot. Pat the scallops dry once more and put them in the pan in a single, uncrowded layer. Let them sear undisturbed until one side is browned and crisp, 2 to 4 minutes. Using tongs, turn the scallops and sear until the second side is well browned and the scallops are firm to the touch. Take the pan off the heat, transfer the scallops on top of the salad. Serve immediately.

Recipe hint

When you're at the fish counter shopping for scallops, you'll often see sea scallops labeled two ways "dry" and "wet." Whenever you can, choose the dry scallops. "Wet" scallops have been treated with a solution called STP (sodium tripolphosphate), which gives scallops a longer shelf life. You'll have trouble browning these scallops, because of the excess moisture. The STP solution can also give scallops a rubbery texture. "Dry" scallops sear better and taste better.

MAKES 6 CUPS SALAD

FOR THE SAUCE

¼ cup low-sodium soy sauce
2 tablespoons light brown sugar
1 tablespoon sherry cooking wine
½ teaspoon sesame oil
1 teaspoon fresh ginger, minced
1 teaspoon garlic, minced

FOR THE SALAD

1 cup broccoli florets
1 cup snow peas
2 cups napa cabbage, chopped
1 cup carrots, cut into match
    sticks
½ cup chow mein noodles
½ cup fresh pineapple, cubed
½ cup peanuts or hazelnuts,
    chopped
½ cup cilantro, chopped

FOR THE SCALLOPS

1 pound large sea scallops
    (about 12) or large shrimp
2 tablespoons extra-virgin olive oil
sea salt and freshly ground black
    pepper

Just another day at the office

SERVES 4

FOR THE CROUTONS

3 ½-inch thick slices French
   bread, crust removed and cut
   into ¾-inch cubes
1 tablespoon extra-virgin olive oil
2 tablespoons butter, melted
3 tablespoons Parmesan cheese,
   grated
2 large garlic cloves, minced

FOR THE CAESAR DRESSING

2 large garlic cloves
3 anchovy fillets
½ teaspoon lemon juice
½ teaspoon Dijon mustard
½ teaspoon Worcestershire sauce
2 teaspoons mayonnaise
⅛ teaspoon sea salt, or as needed
¼ teaspoon freshly ground black
   pepper
¼ cup extra-virgin olive oil

FOR THE SALAD

1 large head romaine lettuce,
   washed, dried and torn into
   pieces
½ cup Parmesan cheese, grated
freshly ground black pepper

FOR THE SALMON

4 (6-ounce) wild salmon fillets,
   skin and pin bones removed

extra-virgin olive oil for grilling
sea salt
freshly ground black pepper

MAKE THE CROUTONS: **Preheat your oven** to 350 degrees. In a large bowl combine the olive oil and butter. Stir in Parmesan cheese and garlic. Add bread cubes and toss until coated. Spread the bread in a single layer on a shallow rimmed baking sheet and sprinkle with a little salt. Bake about 15 minutes or until croutons are golden, stirring once. Set aside.

MAKE THE DRESSING: In a blender, combine the garlic, anchovies, lemon juice, mustard, Worcestershire sauce, mayonnaise, salt and pepper. Mix until well combined. Add oil and blend until smooth.

MAKE THE SALAD: In a large salad bowl, combine lettuce and croutons. Pour dressing over lettuce mixture; toss lightly to coat. Add ¼ cup of the Parmesan and toss well.

MAKE THE SALMON: Preheat a grill or stovetop grill pan to medium-high heat and lightly oil the grates. Season the fillets with salt and pepper. Grill the fillets skinned side up and cook 3 to 5 minutes. Turn fillets over and grill until fish is just cooked through, about 3 minutes more.

Divide Caesar dressing among four plates and top with a salmon fillet. Garnish with Parmesan and serve.

Variations

Use 2 cups purchased croutons. Substitute grilled halibut for the salmon.

Grilled Salmon Caesar Salad with Parmesan Croutons

Whatever its true origins, we're just happy we don't have to go to a restaurant to satisfy our craving for the crunchy, cheesy goodness of a Grilled Salmon Caesar salad!

Crispy Sesame Salad Stack with Orange-Soy Vinaigrette

Impress your family and friends by serving this fashionable salad. Easy enough to prepare during the week and add charm to any special occasion. Make an extra batch of sesame won ton crisps to munch on or to top with your favorite cheese spread for a tasty snack.

MAKE THE VINAIGRETTE: Whisk ¼ cup rice vinegar and next 6 ingredients together in a small bowl until smooth. Season with salt and pepper to taste.

MAKE THE WON TON CRISPS: **Preheat your oven to 400 degrees.** Place won ton wrappers on an ungreased baking sheet. Brush 1 side of each wrapper with melted butter, sprinkle with sesame seeds and salt. Bake 5 to 6 minutes or until golden brown.

MAKE THE SALAD: Layer ½ cup salad greens, 1 sesame won ton crisp, salad greens, 1 sesame won ton crisp and a few mandarin orange segments into the salad greens. Repeat procedure with remaining salad greens, won ton crisps and orange segments. Sprinkle with green onions and cashews. Drizzle with Orange-Soy Vinaigrette. Sprinkle with salt and pepper to taste. Serve immediately.

Recipe hint

Won ton wrappers are fresh pasta sheets that are traditionally stuffed and steamed, boiled, fried or baked. While working with the wrappers, cover the ones you aren't using with a damp towel to keep them moist because they dry out easily. Freeze unused wrappers for up to two months.

SERVES 6

ORANGE-SOY VINAIGRETTE

¼ cup rice vinegar
¼ cup orange juice
2 tablespoons extra-virgin olive oil
1 tablespoon low-sodium soy sauce
2 tablespoons light brown sugar
1 teaspoon freshly grated ginger
¼ teaspoon ground mustard
sea salt and freshly ground black
  pepper to taste

SESAME WON TON CRISPS

12 won ton wrappers (look for them next to the egg roll wrappers and tofu)
1 tablespoon melted butter
1 tablespoon white sesame seeds
1 teaspoon sea salt

SALAD STACK

1 (8-ounce) package mixed salad greens, thoroughly washed
1 (15-ounce) can mandarin oranges, drained
2 green onions, sliced
6 tablespoons cashews, chopped

BLT Salad with Buttermilk Dressing

I will never understand why anyone would want to buy store-bought salad dressing when they are so easy to make, taste far nicer and are not pumped full of preservatives if you make them yourself. I like to make mine in a jam jar so that I can store any left overs easily in the fridge-it will sit quite happily for up to a week, so I often make up double batches to save myself time after a busy day fishing.

SERVES 4

4 slices good-quality bacon
½ baguette, sliced into ¾-inch cubes (or your favorite bread)
2 tablespoons extra-virgin olive oil
sea salt
freshly ground black pepper

FOR THE BUTTERMILK DRESSING

2 tablespoons sour cream
2 tablespoons mayonnaise
1 tablespoons fresh dill, minced
1 tablespoon white vinegar
1 garlic clove, minced
⅓ cup low-fat buttermilk
sea salt
freshly ground black pepper

1 large head Romaine lettuce, washed, dried and torn into pieces
1 cup cherry tomatoes, halved
½ cup Parmesan cheese, grated

Preheat your oven to 375 degrees.

Cook the bacon on a rack-lined baking sheet until crisp, about 15 minutes. Drain on a paper-towel lined plate. Cool, then crumble into large pieces.

Toss bread with oil and season with salt and pepper. Spread evenly on a baking sheet. Bake until golden brown, tossing halfway through, 15 minutes.

MAKE THE BUTTERMILK DRESSING AND ASSEMBLE THE SALAD: In a large bowl whisk together sour cream, mayonnaise, dill, vinegar and garlic. Whisk in buttermilk and season with salt and pepper. Add lettuce, tomatoes and croutons; toss to coat with dressing. Sprinkle with croutons, bacon and Parmesan cheese.

Sandwiches and Pizzas

Serving up a satisfying sandwich or pizza will have you rethinking your next delivery order.

Petersburg

Petersburg was named after Peter Buschmann, a Norwegian immigrant who arrived in the late 1890's and homesteaded on the north end of Mitkof Island. Seeing that the clear, clean ice from the LeConte Glacier could be used to pack fish, he built the Icy Straight Packing Company cannery, a sawmill and a dock. His family's homestead grew into Petersburg, which was populated largely by people of Scandinavian decent.

By 1920, 600 people lived in Petersburg year-round. During this time fresh salmon and halibut were packed in glacial ice for shipment. Alaska's first shrimp processor, Alaskan Glacier, was founded by Earl Ohmer in 1916. A cold storage plant was built by Knut Thompson in 1926. Petersburg's first cannery has operated continuously since and is known as Petersburg Fisheries, a subsidiary of Icicle Seafoods. Petersburg is one of Alaska's major fishing communities.

On May 17th Alaska's Little Norway celebrates the signing of Norway's Constitution in 1814. This annual celebration not only celebrates Norway's Constitution, but U.S. Armed Forces Day, the coming of spring and beginning of the fishing season.

Halibut Burger

When looking for foods that refresh, for something made from your catch and absolutely no time with anything hot in the kitchen, halibut burgers come to mind. Halibut, fillets prized for their unique and meaty texture, when cooked turn incredibly flaky.

MAKES 4 SANDWICHES

4 halibut fillets (4 to 6-ounces each)
    skinned and trimmed
sea salt
freshly ground black pepper
1½ teaspoons ground cumin
⅓ cup extra-virgin olive oil
2 tablespoons lime juice
1 tablespoon minced garlic

FOR THE CUMIN TARTAR

½ cup mayonnaise
1 tablespoon sweet pickle relish
1½ teaspoons Dijon mustard
½ teaspoon ground cumin
½ teaspoon freshly ground black
    pepper
4 sandwich rolls, (such as Ciabatta)
    split and toasted
8 tomato slices
1 cup cilantro leaves

Season halibut fillets with salt, pepper and cumin; place in a shallow dish. Whisk together oil, lime juice and garlic; pour mixture over halibut; turn to coat all sides. Set aside.

MAKE THE TARTAR SAUCE: In a small bowl, blend mayonnaise, relish, mustard, cumin and pepper. Cover and refrigerate until serving.

Heat a grill or stovetop grill pan to medium-high heat and lightly oil the grates. Remove halibut fillets from marinade; place in heated pan and cook, about 3 to 4 minutes, until browned. Turn fillets over and cook just until fish is opaque throughout, about 4 minutes.

Griddle (or toast in oven) cut side of rolls until golden. Spread cut side of each roll with tartar sauce. Place the halibut on the roll bottoms and top with the tomato and cilantro leaves. Cover with roll top.

Grilled Cheese with Bacon, Avocado and Tomato

You will be amazed by how delicious this sandwich is. It is better than a BLT—we predict it will be the best sandwich you've ever tasted!

In a small bowl use a fork to mash together avocado, lemon juice, cumin and salt until smooth. Stir in cilantro and set aside.

Top four of the bread slices with the cheese. Spread with the avocado mixture, tomato slices and 2 bacon slices. Place remaining bread slices on top of the bacon. Spread top of the bread slices lightly with half the butter.

Heat a grill pan or 12-inch skillet over medium-high heat. Carefully add sandwiches, buttered sides down. Carefully spread tops with remaining butter. Cook for 4-6 minutes or until golden, turning once.

MAKES 4 SANDWICHES

- 8 slices good-quality bacon, "cooked"
- 1 avocado, pit removed
- 2½ teaspoons lemon juice
- ½ teaspoon ground cumin
- ¼ teaspoon sea salt
- 2 tablespoons cilantro, chopped
- 8 slices good-quality bread
- 6 ounces Monterey Jack cheese, sliced
- 1 large tomato, thinly sliced
- 2 tablespoons butter, softened

Tenders...

A tender is a large boat that meets the fishermen in a calm cove near the fishing grounds and buys the catch of the day from the fishermen. A tender transports the fish back to the shore-based processing plant. Most fishermen seldom go to town and therefore rely on the tenders for groceries, supplies, ice, fuel and water. This service allows the fishermen to stay on the fishing grounds. The tenders play a vital role in the fishermen's day to day activities and they are much appreciated.

Tony
F/V CHAMPION

Dave
F/V GENE S

AMELIE

Lynn
F/V AMELIE

Perry and Rebecca
F/V ST. JUDE

Poggy and the gang
F/V MICHELE ANN

61041

569611

Orange-Ginger King Crab Salad Sandwich

The phone rang and it was a dear friend of ours asking if we would like king crab for dinner. We jumped to our feet and picked up these beauties! We are blessed to live in such a great land of abundance.

In a small bowl, whisk together the orange zest, orange juice, shallot, ginger, salt, pepper and red pepper flakes. Whisk in the olive oil and sesame oil until emulsified; set aside.

In a large bowl, combine crabmeat, carrots, green onion and the jalapeño. Pour enough of the vinaigrette over the crab mixture to coat and toss to combine.

Cut each croissant vertically. To serve, place bottom half of each croissant on a small plate, top with arugula, crab salad and the top half of the croissant. Cut in half and serve.

Variation Cut each croissant into thirds for a bite-size starter.

MAKES 4

½ teaspoon grated orange zest
3 tablespoons orange juice
1 teaspoon shallot, minced
½ teaspoon grated fresh ginger
¼ teaspoon sea salt
¼ teaspoon ground black pepper
¼ teaspoon red pepper flakes
1 teaspoon extra-virgin olive oil
1 teaspoon sesame oil

½ pound (1½ cups) fresh crabmeat, picked over
½ cup carrots, cut into 1-inch matchsticks
¼ cup green onions, chopped
2 teaspoons jalapeño, seeded and diced
4 large croissants
arugula or leaf lettuce leaves

1 package RapidRise yeast (2¼ tsp.)
½ cup 2% milk
1 cup butter (2 sticks)
   melted, plus more for greasing
3 egg yolks, lightly beaten
¼ cup granulated sugar
2½ cups all-purpose flour
1 teaspoon sea salt

6 eggs
18 slices deli ham
6 slices cheddar cheese
confectioners' sugar, for dusting

MAKE THE ROLLS: In a bowl; combine yeast and ¼ cup water heated to 120 degrees. Let sit until foamy, about 10 minutes. Stir in milk, 4 tablespoons butter and egg yolks until smooth. Add sugar, flour and salt; stir until dough forms. Transfer to a lightly floured work surface; knead until smooth, about 5 minutes. Transfer to a lightly greased bowl, cover with plastic wrap and let rise until doubled, about 1 hour.

Transfer dough to a floured work surface and using a rolling pin, roll into a 18 x 12-inch rectangle. Brush with 2 tablespoons butter; starting at one short end, roll into a cylinder. Cut into 6 equal pieces; transfer, cut side-down, to a parchment-paper-lined baking sheet. Cover with plastic wrap and let rise until doubled. **Preheat your oven** to 375 degrees. Bake until lightly browned, about 15 minutes. Let cool.

MAKE THE SANDWICHES: Heat 2 tablespoons butter in a 12-inch skillet over medium heat. Add 3 eggs, cook and flip until the yolk is just set. Repeat with 2 tablespoons butter and remaining eggs. Split each roll; place 3 slices ham onto each roll bottom. Top with an egg, a slice of cheddar and roll tops. Return skillet to medium-high heat; add 2 tablespoons butter. Add two sandwiches; cook flipping and flattening with a spatula, until browned, about 5 minutes. Repeat with remaining butter and sandwiches. Dust with confectioners' sugar while hot before serving.

PAMELA RAE   PETERSBURG, AK

Ham and Egg Sandwich

While writing this cookbook, I have been thinking about all the delicious treats I've had on my trips out of Alaska. It got me to thinking about the foods that I crave from those travels, which got me to thinking about a trip Ole and I took to Old San Juan. Walking by a bakery, I laid my eyes on a flaky pastry dusted in confectioners' sugar. I had to have one. Fluffy, buttery, slightly sweet and Oh so good! I then learned that you could halve them and stuff each roll with ham, a fried egg and cheese making it a sweet and savory sandwich. I learned to make them and found that this is the sort of recipe that can come together in the evening while watching your favorite show. They will keep well over night and in the morning, you can treat your family to freshly baked sweet rolls.

Guard Island Lighthouse, Ketchikan

Mini Salmon Burger BLTs with Jalapeño Mayo

I have a thing for salmon burgers-they're light and flavorful, easy to make and a nice change from your traditional ground beef burgers. They can work wonders to brighten up any mundane day (they sure do for me). They make great finger food in the summer, by a pool, with a cocktail. There's just something about mini food items isn't there?

Preheat your oven to 375 degrees. Cook the bacon on a rack-lined baking sheet until crisp, about 15 minutes. Drain on a paper-towel lined plate.

MAKE THE PATTIES: In a large bowl, combine salmon, 2 cups bread crumbs, onions and cilantro. Whisk together eggs, lime juice, soy sauce, vinegar, ginger, jalapeño, sugar and salt. Combine with salmon mixture. Form mixture into ten patties; (⅓-cup each) packing each firmly. Press them into the remaining bread crumbs and sesame seeds. Place in freezer until just firm, about 20 minutes.

MAKE THE SAUCE: In a small bowl, stir together jalapeños and mayonnaise.

Heat 2 tablespoons oil in a large nonstick skillet over medium heat. Add salmon patties two at a time; cook until browned on both sides, turning carefully. Transfer the cakes to a plate.

Place the burgers on the roll bottoms and top with the bacon, lettuce, tomato and onion. Spread the roll tops with the sauce and place on the burgers.

Variation

Make larger cakes using a ½ cup measuring cup (makes six) and use regular sized buns.

MAKES 10 PATTIES

5 slices quality thick-cut bacon, cut in half

FOR THE SALMON PATTIES

2 cups wild salmon, cooked, chilled, flaked
2 cups panko bread crumbs, plus ½ to ¾ cup for forming
½ cup green onions, minced
½ cup fresh cilantro, chopped

4 eggs
3 tablespoons lime juice
3 tablespoons low-sodium soy sauce
2 tablespoons rice vinegar
2 tablespoons fresh ginger, minced
2 tablespoons jalapeños, canned or fresh, minced
1 tablespoon granulated sugar
1 teaspoon sea salt

¼ cup sesame seeds
extra-virgin olive oil for frying

FOR THE SAUCE

2 teaspoons jalapeños, canned or fresh, minced
½ cup mayonnaise

FOR THE BURGERS

10 slider buns or brioche rolls, toasted if desired split
crisp lettuce leaves
thinly sliced tomato
thinly sliced onion

Homemade Pizza Dough

After almost twenty years of making pizza, I've learned a thing or two. First – weather effects your dough, it's that plain and simple. On hot days, the dough drinks up the flour, so you will likely need less during the kneading process. Cold wet days, your dough will be moist and will need more flour. Dough that is ready to start the first rise should be smooth and elastic and not at all sticky to the touch. Second – fishermen and people living and working in remote areas LOVE a mouth watering pizza!

MAKES TWO (12-INCH) THIN CRUSTS
OR ONE (16-INCH) THICK CRUST

1 **package RapidRise yeast (2¼ tsp)**
1 **tablespoon granulated sugar**
1¼ **cups warm water (120°)**
3¼ **cups all-purpose flour, divided**
1 **tablespoon extra-virgin olive oil**
2 **teaspoons sea salt**
cornmeal

Home Pizza-Party-Tips

THE PLAN Consider having guests mingle while you share small pizzas, which are best hot from the oven. Put out other foods for them to try as you bake. Figure that each 12-inch pizza will serve one or two people. It's easiest to host a small group-six to eight, for example with one or two topping combinations.

THE TOPPINGS Choose good-quality ready available ingredients, including the freshest vegetables you can find. Prep your toppings, along with balls of dough before guests arrive.

PAIRINGS The drink depends on the occasion and what else you are serving with the pizza. I often serve sparkling red wine that's not too sweet or light-bodied beers work well too.

In a work bowl, combine yeast, sugar and water; let stand for 5 minutes. Using a wooden spoon, add 3 cups of the flour, oil and salt. Stir it together to form a wet, sticky dough. Sprinkle ¼ cup of the remaining flour onto a clean surface, turn dough out and knead for 5 minutes. You may need more or less flour. Place dough in a lightly greased bowl, turning to grease top. Cover and let rise in a warm place (85°), free from drafts, for 45 minutes to 1 hour or until doubled in bulk.

Preheat your oven to 500 degrees. On a lightly floured surface, roll dough out into a 12 or 16-inch circle. Sprinkle a pizza stone or a parchment-paper-lined baking sheet evenly with cornmeal. Place dough on top of stone, folding edges over to form a crust. Prick dough with fork.

Follow instructions for Roasted Garlic and Wild Mushroom Pizza, Artichoke, Tomato and Spinach Pizza, Easy Mozzarella Pizza with Prosciutto and Simple Stromboli.

No time?

Feel free to use store bought bread or pizza dough.

Easy Prosciutto and Mozzarella Pizza

Throw a pizza party and let guests make their own creations with optional topping combinations. Margherita: tomato sauce, fresh mozzarella, basil. Marinara: tomato sauce, oregano, garlic. Ricotta: fresh mozzarella, ricotta, parmigiano, arugula. Sausage: fresh mozzarella, fennel sausage, oven-roasted onions. Fisherman: fresh mozzarella, smoked salmon and dill.

Position a rack in the lower third of the oven and **preheat your oven** to 500 degrees.

On a lightly floured surface, roll dough out into a 12-inch circle. Sprinkle a pizza stone or a parchment-paper-lined baking sheet evenly with cornmeal. Place dough on top of stone, folding edges over to form a crust. Prick dough with fork.

Brush dough lightly with the oil, spread the tomato sauce over dough. Top with olives and cheese slices. Season with pepper. Bake until the crust is a deep golden color and the cheese is bubbly, about 18-20 minutes. Remove from oven and top with prosciutto and fresh basil.

Press out the remaining dough and prepare it using the same directions, so that the second pie will be ready to bake as soon as the first one comes out of the oven. Cut each pizza into 8 slices and serve hot.

MAKES TWO (12-INCH) CRISPY THIN CRUST PIZZA'S

- 1 batch Homemade Pizza Dough, divided into 2 balls
- 1 tablespoon yellow cornmeal
- 2 tablespoons extra-virgin olive oil, divided
- 1 cup marinara, pizza or tomato sauce, divided
- ½ cup pitted black olives, halved, divided
- 1 (8-ounce) ball fresh mozzarella cheese, sliced, divided
- freshly ground black pepper
- 8 thin slices prosciutto, divided
- 2 tablespoons fresh basil leaves, torn, divided

Homemade Pizza Sauce

- 1 tablespoon extra-virgin olive oil
- ½ cup onion, finely chopped
- 3 cloves garlic, minced
- 1 (28-ounce) can crushed tomatoes
- 2 teaspoons Italian seasoning

In a medium saucepan, heat oil over medium heat. Add onion and garlic and cook for 3-4 minutes or until tender. Stir in remaining ingredients; bring to a boil. Reduce heat; simmer for 15 minutes, stirring often.

Artichoke, Tomato and Spinach Pizza

Pizza Saturday has been a ritual on our boat for about seven years now. I usually get the dough started during our last set and prep the rest of the ingredients on the way to the tender to offload our salmon. Everything is ready to go for when we drop anchor. Ole sets up the DVD player and clears the galley table so that once the pies come out of the oven, we can enjoy a pizza and move night. It's such a peaceful way to relax and say goodbye to the hectic week we just finished and get ready for the fishing week ahead.

MAKES ONE 16-INCH PIZZA

5 tablespoons extra-virgin olive oil
6-8 garlic cloves, finely chopped
   (about 3 Tbls.)
sea salt and ground black pepper
1 batch Homemade Pizza Dough
1 tablespoon yellow cornmeal
2 cups shredded mozzarella
½ cup Parmesan cheese, grated,
   divided
1 (13.75-ounce) can artichoke
   hearts, drained and quartered
½ cup sliced black olives
1 cup mushrooms, sliced
½ pint grape tomatoes, halved
2 cups baby spinach, chopped
½ cup fresh basil, julienned

Position a rack in the lower third of the oven and **preheat your oven** to 500 degrees.

In a large bowl, combine the olive oil and garlic. Season with salt and pepper.

On a lightly floured surface, roll dough out into a 16-inch circle. Sprinkle a pizza stone or a parchment-paper-lined baking sheet evenly with cornmeal. Place dough on top of stone, folding edges over to form a crust. Prick dough with fork.

Spread 3 tablespoons of the garlic mixture on top, leaving a ½-inch border, then sprinkle with the mozzarella and ¼ cup of the Parmesan. Toss the artichokes, mushrooms, tomatoes and spinach with the remaining garlic mixture and arrange on top of the cheese. Sprinkle remaining ¼ cup of the Parmesan on top. Place the stone or baking sheet in the oven and bake until the crust is crisp and golden, 18-20 minutes. Top with basil.

Recipe hint

Let the dough rest for 15 minutes if it springs back when you're stretching it to fit the stone or baking sheet.

Roasted Garlic and Mushroom Pizza

The cooked mushroom mixture can be made up to a couple of days ahead and chilled. You can use shiitakes, white button, crimini and oyster mushrooms.

MAKES FOUR (7-INCH) PIZZA'S
OR ONE (16-INCH) THICK CRUST

FOR ROASTED GARLIC

12 garlic cloves (peeled and trimmed)
1 tablespoon extra-virgin olive oil
½ teaspoon red pepper flakes
Toss all together and roast at 375°
until lightly browned (15 minutes)

PIZZA TOPPING

2 tablespoons extra-virgin olive oil
½ medium red onion, thinly sliced
1 pound assorted mushrooms,
   thickly sliced
1 tablespoon fresh oregano, chopped
Roasted Garlic Cloves
sea salt and ground black pepper

1 batch Homemade Pizza Dough,
   divided into 4 balls
2 cups Fontina cheese, grated and
   divided
2 cups mozzarella cheese, grated and
   divided

Position a rack in the lower third of the oven and **preheat your oven** to 500 degrees.

Heat a large sauté pan over medium-high; add olive oil. When hot add the red onion; sauté until translucent.

Add the mushrooms; sauté until lightly browned, about 5 minutes. Stir in oregano and roasted garlic cloves. Continue to cook, stirring until mushrooms are tender. Season with salt and pepper.

Divide dough into 4 pieces; shape into balls, pulling down sides and tucking under as you work around the ball 4 or 5 times. To remove air bubbles, roll each ball under your palm until smooth and firm, about 1 minute.

On a lightly floured surface, roll dough out into a 7 to 8-inch circle, folding edges over to form a crust. Transfer to a pizza stone or a parchment-paper-lined baking sheet dusted with cornmeal, brush the dough with oil and prick with a fork.

Top each crust with ½ cup Fontina cheese, ½ cup mozzarella and ¼ of the mushroom mixture.

Place the stone or baking sheet in the oven and bake until the crust is crisp and golden, 18-20 minutes.

Simple Stromboli

Pizza and Stromboli are the perfect-for-sharing party foods. Everyone loves pizza and everyone has strong opinions about it. People think making pizza is some great mystery, it's like anything else you endeavor to do–it's the process that makes it worthwhile. If certain combinations produce a sandwich you love, chances are that the same combinations will work on a pizza or in a stromboli. Have fun with the toppings, go ahead and experiment.

Preheat your oven to 375 degrees. Line a rimmed baking sheet with parchment paper, brush with oil and sprinkle with cornmeal.

On a lightly floured surface carefully stretch or roll pizza dough to 13 x 10-inch rectangle. Arrange half of the ham slices on dough, leaving a ½-inch border. Sprinkle with ½ cup of the mozzarella cheese. Layer half of the spinach and half of the turkey on cheese. Top with ½ cup of the mozzarella cheese, half the bell pepper, olives and basil. Starting from a long side, roll up into a spiral. Pinch dough to seal seam and ends.

Place dough seam side down, on the prepared baking sheet. Brush with egg. Using a sharp knife, cut slits on top for steam to escape. Quickly roll out the remaining dough and prepare it using the same directions. Bake about 30 minutes or until golden. Let stand 10 minutes. To serve, cut loaf into serving size pieces.

MAKES TWO STROMBOLI

2 teaspoons extra-virgin olive oil, divided
1 tablespoon yellow cornmeal, divided
1 batch Homemade Pizza Dough, divided into 2 balls
8 ounces thinly sliced cooked ham, divided
2 cups mozzarella cheese, shredded, divided
2 cups fresh baby spinach, divided
8 ounces thinly sliced cooked turkey, divided
⅔ cup red bell pepper, chopped, divided
½ cup Kalamata olives, pitted, chopped, divided
½ cup fresh basil, chopped, divided
1 egg lightly beaten

Starters and Party Foods

Perfect for cocktail parties, potlucks or just a night at home in front of the tv. These little nibbles and dips are more than just quick. They turn last minute gatherings into flavor adventures.

∾∾∾∾∾∾∾∾∾∾

Sitka

The sea-side community is thought to be the most beautiful of Southeast Alaska cities. It's the only town in Southeast Alaska that faces the Gulf of Alaska head on. Nestled on the west side of Baranof Island, it is flanked on the east by majestic snow capped mountains and on the west by the Pacific Ocean. The name Sitka is derived from Sheet'ká, a contraction of the Tlingit name Shee Atiká, meaning "People on the Outside of Shee" (Baranof Island). The Sitka National Historic Park is Alaska's oldest national park established in 1910 to commemorate the 1804 Battle of Sitka, as well as to preserve Native totemic art.

In 1741, the Vitus Berring expedition recorded the location of the Tlingit settlement at Sitka and recognized the value of the location and resources, recording this in their log books. The world of the Tlingit people came to a turning point in 1799 when the Russians returned, built a fort and trading post and named the site "New Archangel." In 1802, the Tlingit destroyed the Russian outpost, however the Russians returned in 1804 and retaliated by destroying the Tlingit fort in the Battle of Sitka. Just a few years later, in 1808, Sitka became the capital of Russian-America, a vast territory that extended from Northern Alaska, south to Fort Ross, California. When the United States purchased Alaska from Russia in 1867 for $7.2 million, the Stars and Stripes were first raised on Castle Hill in downtown Sitka. Sitka was the capital of the Alaska Territory until 1906 when it was moved to Juneau.

Cheese Straws

Don't let the delicate look of these hors d'oeuvres fool you. A touch of cayenne gives them a hint of heat that makes them a tasty accompaniment to a pre-dinner cocktail party. You will be amazed with how quickly they disappear!

MAKES 20

2 sheets (1 box) frozen puff pastry defrosted overnight in the refrigerator
1 large egg
½ cup Parmesan cheese, grated
1 cup sharp cheddar cheese, grated
2 teaspoons fresh thyme leaves, minced
1 teaspoon sea salt
⅛ teaspoon ground cayenne or to taste

Preheat your oven to 375 degrees.

Line two baking sheets with parchment paper.

Roll out each sheet of puff pastry on a lightly floured board until it's 10 by 12-inches. Beat the egg with 1 tablespoon of water and brush the surface of the pastry. Sprinkle each sheet evenly with ¼ cup of Parmesan, ½ cup of the cheddar, 1 teaspoon of the thyme, ½ teaspoon of the salt and some of the cayenne pepper.

With the rolling pin, lightly press the flavorings into the puff pastry. With the long side closest to you, using a floured knife or pizza wheel, cut each sheet in half vertically. Then cut each sheet horizontally into five 1-inch strips. Twist each strip and lay on baking sheets. Bake for 10 minutes, until lightly browned and puffed. Turn each straw and bake for another 2 minutes. Don't over bake or the cheese will burn. Cool and serve at room temperature.

Chipotle and Rosemary Roasted Nuts

Ground chipotle pepper is a course red powder that is so easy-to-use it almost feels like cheating. Chipotle makes an attractive tabletop shaker for pizzas, tacos, salads or sprinkle a little on mixed nuts for a sweet, salty and spicy treat.

Preheat your oven to 350 degrees.

Line a rimmed baking sheet with parchment paper.

In a large bowl, combine the mixed nuts with the olive oil, maple syrup, brown sugar, orange juice and chipotle powder; tossing to coat. Add 2 tablespoons of the rosemary and toss again.

Spread the nuts in one layer. Roast for 25 minutes, stirring twice with a large spatula, until the nuts are glazed and golden brown. Remove from the oven and sprinkle with salt and the remaining 2 tablespoons of rosemary. Toss well and set aside at room temperature, stirring occasionally to prevent sticking as they cool. Serve warm or cool completely and store in airtight containers at room temperature for up to a week.

SERVES 4-6 AS A STARTER

7 to 8 cups mixed nuts
2 tablespoons extra-virgin olive oil
⅓ cup maple syrup
¼ cup firmly packed light brown sugar
3 tablespoons orange juice
2 teaspoons ground chipotle powder
4 tablespoons fresh rosemary, minced and divided
sea salt, if desired

Spicy Tomato Salsa

This salsa is bursting with tons of fresh flavors and couldn't be any easier or quicker to make. Just put everything into a food processor and pulse to your desired consistency. Then sit down with an entire bag of tortilla chips and a bowl of this salsa and watch them both disappear. It's amazing how quickly that can happen, right?

Combine all of the ingredients in a serving bowl, cover and refrigerate until chilled. Serve with tortilla chips or Toasted Pita Chips.

Recipe hint

Capsaicin - the chemical that gives chili peppers their burn - is dangerous to the skin and eyes, so handle them with gloves or oiled hands. Don't cut on wooden surfaces or under running water and process at arms length. Counteract the burning with a bit of sugar or a sip of a dairy product.

MAKES ABOUT 4 CUPS

2 cups tomatoes, diced
½ cup onion, diced
2 teaspoons garlic, minced
1-2 jalapeño peppers, seeded, minced
3 tablespoons cilantro, minced
1 (8-ounce) can tomato sauce
1 tablespoon granulated sugar
1 tablespoon lemon juice
1 tablespoon white vinegar
2 tablespoons extra-virgin olive oil
½ teaspoon dried oregano
1 teaspoon sea salt
tortilla chips or Toasted Pita Chips (page 101) for serving.

> **Did you know?** The State Seal was originally designed in 1910 while Alaska was a territory and not a state.
>
> The rays above the mountains represent the northern lights. The smelter symbolizes mining. The train stands for Alaska's railroads and ships denote transportation by sea. The tree symbolize Alaska's wealth of forests and the farmer, his horse and the three shocks of wheat represent Alaskan agriculture. The fish and the seals signify the importance of fishing and wildlife to Alaska's economy.

Perfect Guacamole

There are a few dishes as simple yet easily varied as guacamole. This version lets the flavor and texture of the avocados shine through, amply reinforced with cilantro, green onions and a splash of lemon juice. It can be set out as a dip, used as a garnish for tacos or chili or spread on sandwiches and burgers.

MAKES ABOUT 2 CUPS

3 large firm-ripe avocados, pit removed
1 tablespoon lemon juice
4 cloves garlic, minced
3 green onions, chopped
¼ cup fresh cilantro, chopped
⅓ cup fresh or store-bought salsa, drained
⅓ cup canned jalapeño peppers, drained, chopped
⅓ cup black olives, drained and finely chopped (optional)
½ cup sour cream
sea salt to taste
2 tablespoons crumbled feta cheese
tortilla chips or Toasted Pita Chips (page 101) for serving

Recipe hint

Avocado flesh discolors quickly. To keep your guacamole from turning brown, add an avocado pit. You could also cover avocado dishes with lemon or lime slices or tightly pressed plastic wrap.

Put the avocado in a bowl and coarsely mash with a fork. Stir in the lemon juice along with the garlic, green onions, cilantro, salsa, jalapeño's and olives. Fold in the sour cream. Season to taste with salt.

Heap the guacamole into a bowl and garnish it with feta cheese. Serve with tortilla chips or Toasted Pita Chips.

Artichoke Hummus with Toasted Pita Chips

Hummus is seriously one of my favorite things to make. It takes approximately 5.73 minutes... okay maybe 10 minutes, if you take your time opening the can of garbanzo beans and artichoke hearts... and it's a delicious and healthy snack. If you do make this, it's very possible you will never stop eating it!

In a bowl of a food processor, combine all ingredients; process until smooth. Serve with Toasted Pita Chips.

TOASTED PITA CHIPS

4 pita bread rounds, cut into triangles
2 tablespoons extra-virgin olive oil
½ teaspoon sea salt

Preheat your oven to 400 degrees.

Brush both sides of the triangles with olive oil Place on a baking sheet lined with parchment paper and sprinkle tops with salt. Bake for 5 minutes or until lightly brown. Cool completely; store in an airtight container.

MAKES ABOUT 3 CUPS

1 (16-ounce) canned chickpeas, drained
1 (14-ounce) can marinated artichoke hearts, drained
½ cup tahini paste
6 tablespoons extra-virgin olive oil
3 tablespoons lemon juice
2 tablespoons fresh parsley, chopped
1 teaspoon minced garlic
1 teaspoon sea salt
1 teaspoon paprika
¼ teaspoon ground cayenne
⅛ teaspoon ground black pepper

Did you know? Pregnant Steller sea lions give birth soon after arriving on a rookery, and copulation generally occurs one to two weeks after giving birth, but the fertilized egg does not become implanted in the uterus until the fall. Twins are rare. After a week or so of nursing without leaving the rookery, females begin to take progressively longer and more frequent foraging trips, leaving their pups behind, until at some point in late summer the mother and pup both leave the rookery.

Crab Croquettes

There are so many small-bites we have created and fine tuned and I love sharing them with you. To me, crab croquettes are about two things-sweet crabmeat and a crispy batter. Dungeness crabmeat is a must, if you can get it. Truly addictive, light and airy, it may not make it out of your kitchen. You'll want to eat it immediately!

MAKES 18-20

FOR THE CROQUETTES

2 cups fresh Dungeness crabmeat
(about 2 crab, cooked and cleaned)
1 cup panko bread crumbs
¼ cup green onions, minced
1 tablespoon fresh parsley, chopped
2 tablespoons grated lemon zest
2 tablespoons lemon juice
⅓ cup mayonnaise
1¼ teaspoons Old Bay seasoning
1 teaspoon Worcestershire sauce
¼ teaspoon ground cayenne
½ teaspoon ground mustard

FOR THE BATTER

4 egg yolks
½ cup 2% milk
½ cup cold club soda or beer
2¼ teaspoons Old Bay seasoning
1 cup all-purpose flour
2 teaspoons baking powder
vegetable oil (about 4 cups) for frying
Mae Ploy sweet chili sauce for serving

MAKE THE CRAB CROQUETTES: In a large bowl gently combine crabmeat through mustard.

MAKE THE BATTER: In a small bowl, whisk together egg yolks, milk, club soda and Old Bay seasoning. Add the flour and baking powder and gently stir until the batter is just combined.

Heat 2-inches of oil in 3-quart straight-sided heavy-bottomed pan over medium heat until it reaches 350° degrees on a deep-fat thermometer.

Form crab mixture into "cocktail size" balls. (About one slightly heaping tablespoon each). Place the crab ball on a slotted spoon and coat with the batter. (Let the excess batter drain off). Carefully lay them into the hot oil. Turn the croquettes frequently until golden brown. Remove croquettes to a paper-towel lined plate. Serve immediately. Dip in Mae Ploy, if desired.

Recipe hint

Fry croquettes a few at a time. Adding too many at a time will drop the oil's heat, resulting in greasy fluffs.

Pancetta Wrapped King Salmon Kebabs

You could wrap just about anything in bacon and I would devour it. But bacon wrapped salmon? Could it possibly get more mouth watering?

Heat a grill or stovetop grill pan to medium heat.

MAKE THE ROSEMARY OIL: In a small saucepan, heat the olive oil, rosemary and garlic over medium-low heat until the garlic sizzles and begins to brown around the edges, about 3 minutes. Remove the pan from the heat and stir in the red pepper flakes. Divide oil between two small bowls with a rosemary sprig in each and let cool to room temperature.

MAKE THE SALMON: In a large bowl, combine remaining tablespoon oil and salmon. Toss to coat. Sprinkle the salmon with salt and a few grinds of black pepper. On a work surface, set out rows of 3 salmon chunks. Unroll pancetta slices into strips. Working with one chunk at a time, wrap strips once or twice around salmon. Skewer each row of salmon with chunks slightly separated.

Brush grill grate with oil. Place kebabs on grate, cook turning once, until fish flakes easily with a fork. Place kebabs on plates and serve with rosemary oil.

SERVES 4 AS A STARTER

FOR THE ROSEMARY OIL

¼ cup extra-virgin olive oil
  plus 1 tablespoon for grill
2 fresh rosemary sprigs
2 cloves garlic, thinly sliced
⅛ teaspoon crushed red pepper
  flakes

FOR THE SALMON

¼ teaspoon sea salt
¼ teaspoon freshly ground black
  pepper
1½ pounds king, coho or sockeye
  salmon, skin and pin bones
  removed, cut into 1½-inch
  chunks
4 ounces pancetta, thinly sliced

Naturally Better Salmon in general is touted as a nutritional powerhouse, but wild salmon takes the benefits over the top. On average wild salmon has 20 percent more protein and 20 percent less fat than farm-raised salmon. What's more, the fat in wild salmon is much higher in Omega-3 fatty acids than its captive counterpart (Omega-3's contribute to a healthy heart, among many other benefits). It makes sense that a demanding life cycle produces a fitter fish. Swimming in icy ocean currents and eating a wide variety of sea life naturally produces a vigorous nutrient-rich, high-protein, low fat salmon. It's pricier to bring to the market, but its high nutritional quality makes it a value to catch.

Roasted Shrimp with Rosemary and Thyme

This is the perfect recipe for shrimp. Roasting them with fresh rosemary and thyme adds so much flavor. I am positive you will love this recipe and will never serve shrimp other than this way again.

SERVES 4 AS A STARTER
OR 2 AS A MAIN COURSE

½ cup extra-virgin olive oil
3 large fresh rosemary sprigs, halved
4 fresh thyme sprigs
freshly ground black pepper
1½ pounds medium shrimp, peeled, leaving tails intact
½ teaspoon sea salt

Preheat your oven to 400 degrees.

Pour the oil into a 9 x 13-inch rimmed baking dish. Add the rosemary, thyme and 1 teaspoon pepper and bake until the mixture is fragrant, about 10 minutes.

Add the shrimp to the dish and toss with tongs until coated. Bake the shrimp until pink and firm about 10 minutes.

Add a sprinkling of salt, toss well and serve.

Crab Stuffed Mushrooms

Crab stuffed mushrooms only look difficult to make. A large tray with an army of mini-sized appetizers, each little soldier with a browned bubbling cheese crust, only suggests that you've slaved over them for days. Really, the most work you've done is chop up some vegetables and spoon filling into some mushroom caps, my favorite kind of appetizer!

Preheat your oven to 425 degrees.

In a skillet, cook the bacon over medium-high heat until crisp. Remove to a paper-towel lined plate.

Place mushroom caps, hollow side up, on a rimmed baking sheet that has been lined with parchment paper.

In a medium bowl, combine cream cheese and heavy cream. Add garlic, shallots, spinach, 4 tablespoons Parmesan cheese, lemon juice, Worcestershire and chili sauce. Season with salt and pepper. Gently stir in diced bacon and crab.

In a small bowl, toss bread crumbs with the olive oil, 3 tablespoons Parmesan cheese, salt and pepper to taste.

Stuff mushrooms by dividing crab filling evenly into each cap. Top with the crumbs, pressing lightly. Bake 8 to 10 minutes until heated through and topping is golden. Serve immediately.

Variation

Feel free to substitute medium size shrimp in place of the crab.

MAKES 24

- 3 slices good-quality bacon, diced
- 24 medium sized mushroom caps, hollowed
- 2 cups fresh Dungeness crabmeat (about 2 crab, cooked and cleaned)
- ⅓ cup cream cheese, softened
- ¼ cup heavy cream
- 3 garlic cloves, minced
- 1 shallot, minced
- 1½ cups baby spinach, chopped
- 4 tablespoons Parmesan cheese, grated
- 1 teaspoon lemon juice
- 1 teaspoon Worcestershire sauce
- ⅛ teaspoon hot chili sauce
- sea salt and freshly ground black pepper to taste

- ½ cup fresh bread crumbs, crust removed and cut into ¼-inch cubes
- 2 tablespoons extra-virgin olive oil
- 3 tablespoons Parmesan cheese, finely grated
- sea salt and freshly ground black pepper to taste

Garlic Shrimp Crostini

This is one of my favorite appetizers to make. It's simple, fancy and tastes amazing!

MAKES 24

1 (8-ounce) package cream
   cheese, softened

¼ cup mayonnaise

5 cloves garlic, minced and
   divided

1 tablespoon green onion,
   minced

pinch of sea salt

¼ cup butter

1 tablespoon fresh parsley,
   minced

1 pound medium shrimp,
   peeled, leaving tails intact

24 toasted baguette slices,
   (Preheat oven to 350˚. Brush both
   sides with olive oil and season
   with sea salt. Bake until golden)

Garnish: halved cherry tomatoes,
fresh parsley leaves

In a small bowl, combine cream cheese, mayonnaise, 2 cloves garlic and green onions; set aside.

In a large skillet, melt butter over medium heat. Add remaining 3 cloves garlic and parsley; cook for 3 minutes. Add shrimp; cook for 3 to 4 minutes or until pink and firm.

Spread cream cheese mixture evenly over bread rounds. Top each with 1 shrimp. Garnish with tomato halves and parsley leaves.

Make ahead

The cream cheese spread can be made the day before to save time. You can bake the crostini toast up to a week in advance.

Variation

Instead of standing the shrimp up, take the tails off and lay them on their sides. It makes them a little easier to eat. Adding a small slice of avocado is extra yummy. Feel free to substitute crab or lobster for the shrimp.

Crab Salad on Corn Blini

Cornmeal with it's pleasant flavor and slightly crunchy texture, makes this little bite lip smacking pop it in your mouth good! I'll bet you can't eat just one!

MAKE THE SALAD: In a medium bowl, gently toss together the crabmeat, bell pepper, chives, Dijon, 1 tablespoon mayonnaise, ¼ teaspoon salt and pepper until mixture is well combined. Refrigerate.

In the bowl of a food processor, combine the avocado, remaining mayonnaise, lime juice, half the jalapeño slices, remaining salt and pulse until the mixture is smooth.

MAKE THE CORN BLINI: In a small bowl, combine the yeast and water and let stand until foamy, about 5 minutes. In a medium bowl, stir together the cornmeal, flour and salt. Add the milk, butter and yeast mixture, whisk until smooth. Let the mixture sit uncovered, at room temperature for 10 minutes.

Heat a nonstick skillet over medium heat; when hot, spray the pan with nonstick cooking spray. Working in batches of three, spoon 1 tablespoon batter into skillet for each blini and cook 2 to 3 minutes on each side until crisp around the edges and golden brown. Transfer to a plate and cover with foil to keep the blini warm.

Top each corn blini with crab salad; garnish with avocado purée and remaining jalapeño slices, if desired.

MAKES 12-16

FOR THE SALAD

- ½ pound (1½ cups) fresh crabmeat, picked over
- ¼ cup red bell pepper, finely chopped
- 2 tablespoons chives, minced
- 1½ teaspoons Dijon mustard
- 3 tablespoons mayonnaise, divided
- ½ teaspoon sea salt, divided
- ¼ teaspoon ground black pepper
- 1 avocado, pit removed
- 2 tablespoons lime juice
- 1 small jalapeño, cut in half lengthwise, seeded and thinly sliced, divided

FOR THE CORN BLINI

- 1 teaspoon RapidRise yeast
- 2 tablespoons warm water (120°)
- ½ cup yellow cornmeal
- ½ cup all-purpose flour
- ¼ teaspoon sea salt
- ½ cup 2% milk
- 3 tablespoons butter, melted

Prosciutto-Wrapped Nectarine Bites

This riff on a classic Italian hors d'oeuvre is a great way to start a gathering. You might want to double the recipe-they disappear fast!

MAKES 16

¼ cup orange marmalade
2 tablespoons white vinegar
½ teaspoon red pepper flakes
4 nectarines, halved, pitted
8 slices prosciutto, cut in half lengthwise
16 fresh basil leaves
½ pound fresh mozzarella, sliced

Coat the grates of a grill or stovetop grill pan with nonstick spray, then preheat to medium-high heat.

In a small saucepan, heat the marmalade, vinegar and pepper flakes about 3 minutes. Remove from heat.

Grill nectarine halves cut side down for 5 minutes. Cut each in half again.

Working with one nectarine at a time, secure a basil leaf and a mozzarella slice, positioning it so that it will peek out from the prosciutto when rolled. Roll the nectarine up in the prosciutto. Drizzle each with marmalade mixture and serve.

Make ahead

You can assemble these up to 2 hours ahead if you like, but the basil may darken a bit.

Basil tip

Here's how to keep fresh basil at it's best for several days. Wrap basil in slightly damp paper towels and refrigerate in a plastic bag up to 4 days. Or place basil, stems down, in a glass of water and cover the leaves with a plastic bag; refrigerate up to 7 days, changing the water every couple of days.

Variation

Substitute half of 1 small cantaloupe or honeydew for the nectarine.

Do Fishermen Make a Good Catch...

The answer is Yes!
Here are my top 15 reasons why I think they're awesome.

1. They are cute in their sweat shirts, rain gear, Xtratufs and baseball hats.

2. They are in great physical shape and love the challenges presented by the sea.

3. They know how to bring home the bacon.

4. They don't mind the five o'clock shadow and neither do I.

5. They are good listeners and always have a good story to tell.

6. They are patient and willing to lend a hand.

7. They brave through rough storms, pain and sleep deprivation to get the job done.

8. They are self sufficient and can fix anything.

9. They can survive a storm that knocks out their navigation and with their amazing sense of direction find their way home.

10. They are open minded and willing to take advise.

11. They fish in the harshest conditions without complaining.

12. They are driven and do whatever it takes, instead of relying on luck to fill their holds.

13. They love a home cooked meal and dessert while at sea.

14. They work hard, play hard and love to go on vacation.

15. They love their families and are excited to come home!

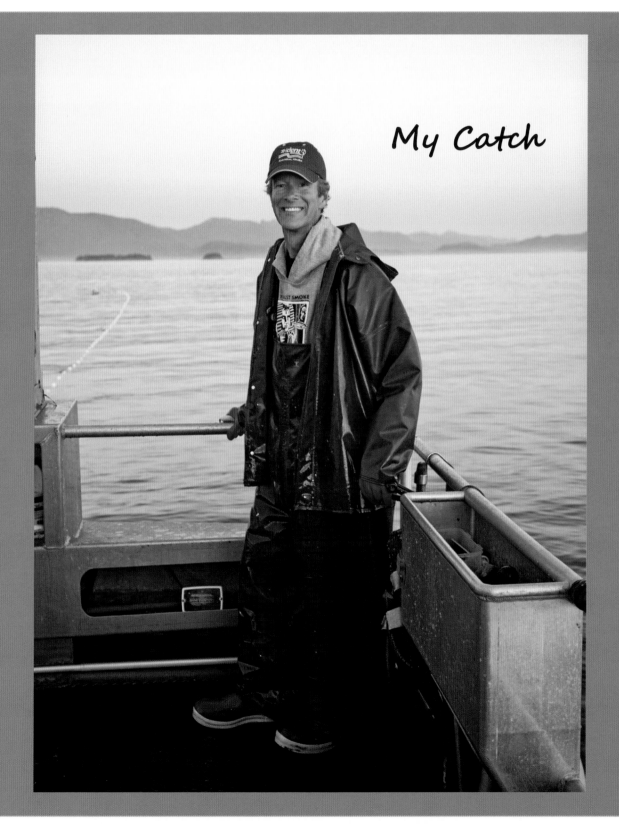

My Catch

Pan-Fried Oysters
with Tartar Sauce

Ole loves the intense flavor of oysters and like most fishermen, he adores anything fried. These are hands-down the best pan fried oysters I have ever made. You might want to double the recipe, you'll be wishing you had more!

SERVES 2-4 AS A STARTER

FOR THE TARTAR SAUCE

2 cups mayonnaise
⅓ cup celery, minced
⅓ cup onion, minced
2 tablespoons lemon juice
1 tablespoon Worcestershire
    sauce
pinch sea salt
pinch ground mustard
pinch ground black pepper
2 tablespoons dill pickle relish

FOR THE OYSTERS

2 dozen shucked oysters,
    drained well
⅓ cup all-purpose flour
1 teaspoon sea salt
1 teaspoon ground black pepper
¼ cup extra-virgin olive oil
lemon wedges

MAKE THE TARTAR SAUCE: Combine all ingredients and mix well.

MAKE THE OYSTERS: Season the flour with salt and pepper and coat the oysters well, shaking off the excess.

Heat the oil in a 10 to 12-inch sauté pan, just until it begins to smoke. If the oil is too hot, the oysters will burn. If the oil is too cool, the oysters will be soggy.

Slip the floured oysters into the hot oil and shake a little to keep them separated. Pan-fry for 1 to 2 minutes, turn and fry 1 to 2 minutes on the other side. The oysters should be crisp and golden brown on both sides. Remove oysters with a slotted spoon or spatula and drain on paper towels. Serve the oysters with lemon wedges and tartar sauce.

Recipe hint

When possible, buy local shucked oysters. Oysters are also available at most grocery stores in the seafood department in 10-ounce jars. The jars indicate whether the oysters are extra small, small or medium.

Coconut Shrimp with Green Goddess Dip

I love, love, love coconut shrimp. In fact anything that reminds me of a tropical get-away or a summer night is perfect in my book. Just put on some Jimmy Buffett, Bob Marley or any steel drum band and I am in my own personal heaven. Now where did I put my Piña Colada?

MAKE THE DIP: Combine all ingredients except salt and pepper in a blender until smooth. Season with salt and pepper. Cover and refrigerate until ready to use.

MAKE THE SHRIMP: Rinse and pat dry, sprinkle with salt. On a large plate, mix together flour and coconut. Dip each shrimp into egg whites, then roll in the coconut mixture. In a large skillet over medium-high heat, add about ¼-inch oil. When oil is sizzling, carefully add 3 to 4 shrimp at a time and cook until coconut is golden brown, about 2 minutes per side. Remove shrimp with a slotted spoon and transfer to a paper-towel lined plate.

Alternative: Caribbean Dipping Sauce

1 tablespoon butter
2 teaspoons minced garlic
2 teaspoons grated fresh ginger
1 jalapeño pepper, seeded and minced
1 (18-ounce) jar orange marmalade
3 tablespoons lime juice
1 tablespoon whole-grain mustard
1 teaspoon prepared horseradish
¼ teaspoon sea salt

In a medium saucepan, melt butter over medium-high heat. Add garlic, ginger and jalapeño pepper; Cook for 2 minutes, stirring constantly. Reduce heat to medium-low. Add marmalade, lime juice, mustard, horseradish and salt. Simmer for 5 minutes, stirring frequently. Serve warm.

SERVES 4 AS A STARTER

GREEN GODDESS DIP

½ cup mayonnaise
½ cup sour cream
¼ cup low-fat buttermilk
3 tablespoons white vinegar
1 teaspoon anchovy paste
    or 1-2 anchovy fillets
2 garlic cloves
1 teaspoon Dijon mustard
2 tablespoons fresh basil leaves
2 tablespoons fresh dill
2 tablespoons fresh Italian
    parsley
2 tablespoons fresh mint leaves
sea salt and freshly ground black
    pepper

FOR THE SHRIMP

1 pound medium shrimp, peeled,
    leaving tails intact
½ teaspoon sea salt
2 cups flaked coconut
3 tablespoons all-purpose flour
2 teaspoons Caribbean jerk
    seasoning, optional
2-3 egg whites lightly, whisked
extra-virgin olive oil, for frying

MAKES 12

FOR THE GRIT CAKES

2¼ cups low-sodium organic
   chicken broth
1 tablespoons butter
½ teaspoon sea salt
¾ cup uncooked coarse-ground
   yellow corn grits
3 tablespoons shallot, minced
3 tablespoons fresh basil leaves,
   chopped
½ cup Parmesan cheese, grated
2 (3-ounce) packages thinly
   sliced wild smoked salmon
garnish: ½ cup mixed berries, fresh
basil sprigs

FOR THE MIXED BERRY SPREAD

½ cup fresh blueberries
½ cup fresh blackberries
½ cup fresh raspberries or
   salmonberries
⅓ cup granulated sugar
½ teaspoon vanilla extract
½ cup cream cheese, softened
1 teaspoon grated lemon zest

Recipe hint

Grits are confusing to both the Southerner and non-Southerner alike, so let me break it down for you. The word "grit" is a shortened way of saying what it really means, "hominy grits." Grits are derived from hominy. Hominy is dried corn kernels with the hull and germ removed. When this dried hominy is ground, it turns into what we know as grits.

MAKE THE GRIT CAKES: Spray a 9 x 13-inch baking dish with cooking spray. In a medium saucepan over medium-high heat, bring the broth, butter and salt to a boil. Gradually whisk in grits and cook 1 minute. Reduce heat to medium and simmer until grits are thick, whisking frequently, 6 to 8 minutes. Add the shallot, basil and Parmesan and cook for an additional 2 minutes.

Pour cooked grits into the prepared baking dish. Press a piece of plastic wrap directly onto the surface of the grits; refrigerate for two hours or until firm. Unmold chilled grits onto a large cutting board. Cutting the grits into 12 (2¼-inch) cakes.

MAKE THE MIXED BERRY SPREAD: In a small saucepan over medium heat, combine the berries, sugar and vanilla and cook until mixture is thickened, about 8 minutes. Remove from heat and cool slightly. Pour berry mixture into a food processor and blend until liquefied. Strain through a fine-mesh sieve; discard seeds. In a small bowl, using an electric mixer, blend together the strained berry mixture, cream cheese and lemon zest until well combined. Chill until ready to use.

In a large nonstick skillet over medium-high heat, sear each cake 2 minutes per side or until lightly browned and heated through. Remove from heat and cool slightly. Spread an even layer of the mixed berry spread onto each grit cake, then top with a slice of the smoked salmon, trimming salmon if necessary. Garnish with a dollop of the mixed berry spread, a few berries and a sprig of basil.

Smoked Salmon with Wild Berries on Grit Cakes

This recipe makes a terrific, simple yet sophisticated appetizer-perfect for cocktail hour. The berry spread brings out the richness of the smoked salmon, which is complemented by the slight sweetness of the grit cakes. It is one of our go-to appetizers when we want something truly satisfying.

Bacon-Wrapped Dates

Everything tastes better with bacon and dates are no exception! This appetizer is simple to make and can be prepared before the party, so your guests will be munching on the salty, sweet and oh-so-satisfying bite-sized, bacon-wrapped dates the second they arrive at your home.

Preheat your oven to 350 degrees.

Wrap each date with one-third slice bacon and secure with a toothpick.

In a small bowl, mix together soy sauce, brown sugar, and lemon juice. Dip each bacon-wrapped date into sauce, coating well. Place on a rimmed baking sheet lined with parchment paper and bake for 20 minutes or until done. Serve warm.

MAKES 24

- 24 dried dates, pit removed
- 8 slices good-quality bacon, sliced into thirds
- ½ cup low-sodium soy sauce
- 2 tablespoons light brown sugar
- 2 tablespoons lemon juice

Recipe hint To help prevent the toothpicks from burning in the oven, soak them in water before skewing appetizers.

Did you know? The bald eagle is named for its conspicuous white head and tail. The distinctive white adult plumage is not attained until 5 or more years of age. Immature birds lack this easily identifiable characteristic and can be confused with the golden eagle. The immature bald eagle's unfeathered tarsi (lower legs) and whitish wing linings on the forward part of the wings can be helpful distinctions where the two species coexist. The bald eagle is Alaska's largest bird of prey with a wing span up to 7½ feet and weights of 8 to 14 pounds. Like many raptors, females are larger than males. Bald eagles often use the same nest each year. Nest trees are usually close to water, afford a clear view of the surrounding area and offer sparse cover above the nest. Fish are the main diet of the bald eagle. There is a misconception that eagles cannot let go of prey. The talons grasp, but it's purely voluntary. An eagle will sometimes grab a fish that's too heavy to lift and will choose to swim, towing the meal to shore, rather than loose it.

Steamed Clams with Spicy Sausage and Garlic

What could be easier to make and more delicious than steamed clams? I can't think of anything else!

SERVES 4 AS A STARTER
OR 2 AS A MAIN COURSE

3 tablespoons butter
½ cup onion, chopped
3 cloves garlic, chopped
½ cup yellow bell pepper,
   chopped
1 cup dry white wine
½ teaspoon cumin seeds
2-3 pounds little neck clams,
   scrubbed
½ cup spicy cured pork sausage,
   cubed
freshly ground black pepper
2 tablespoons cilantro
melted butter for serving
thick slices of French bread

Melt the butter in a large pot over medium heat. Sauté the onion, garlic and bell pepper until soft. Add the white wine and cumin seeds and bring to a slow boil. Add clams and sausage and cover pot with a tight fitting lid. Steam over low heat just until clams open, about 5 to 10 minutes. Do not over cook as clams will become tough and rubbery. (Discard any clams that are not open). Season with pepper and stir in cilantro.

Use tongs or a slotted spoon to transfer the clams to individual bowls with individual cups of melted butter.

Pour broth through a cheesecloth-lined strainer to remove any sand. The broth can be used as a dunking liquid for the French bread.

Recipe hint

Cilantro, also called Chinese parsley, is used a great deal in Asian and Latin American cooking. It cools spicy foods and has a unique flavor and aroma.

Crab, Shrimp and Pork Pot Stickers

I absolutely love eating pot stickers. What's not to love about them? Crispy on one side, tender on the other and bursting with a flavorful crab, shrimp and pork filling. These are simple to assemble and sheer gold sitting in your freezer! The uncooked pot stickers can be placed on a parchment lined tray (make sure they're not touching) and freeze. Transfer to a plastic freezer bag and store for up to a month. To cook the frozen pot stickers, add an extra minute to the cooking time after the water is added.

MAKE THE SAUCE: Combine all and serve in a small bowl.

MAKE THE FILLING: Combine all in a medium-size bowl until just combined.

MAKE THE DUMPLINGS: Put a **level** tablespoon of filling in the center of each round, then brush half way around the edge with a little water and fold in half, pressing edges together to seal, leaving a small opening at each end of semicircle. As they are completed, place the pot sticker on a parchment paper-lined tray. Continue with remaining wrappers.

Heat peanut oil in a 12-inch **nonstick** skillet over medium heat until hot, then remove from heat and arrange dumplings in a tight circular pattern seam side up in oil (they should touch one another). Cook, uncovered, over medium heat until oil sizzles, then drizzle warm water over pot stickers and cook, covered, until pot sticker bottoms are browned, 8 to 10 minutes. Add 2 tablespoons more water if skillet looks dry before bottoms are browned. Remove lid and cook, shaking skillet to loosen pot stickers, until steam dissipates. Invert a large plate with a rim over skillet. Using pot holders, hold plate and skillet together and invert skillet. Remove skillet and serve pot stickers warm with dipping sauce.

Make ahead

Pot stickers can be formed 4 hours ahead. Chill in 1 layer, not touching, on a parchment paper-lined tray, loosely but completely covered with plastic wrap.

MAKES 24

FOR THE DIPPING SAUCE

1/3 cup low-sodium soy sauce
2 tablespoons rice vinegar
2 tablespoons water
1 teaspoon granulated sugar
1 green onion, minced

FOR THE FILLING

1/2 cup fresh crabmeat, picked over
1/2 cup peeled raw shrimp, coarsely chopped
1/4 pound unseasoned ground pork
6 water chestnuts, rinsed and diced
1/2 cup green onion, chopped
1 1/2 tablespoons low-sodium soy sauce
2 teaspoons fresh ginger, minced
1 teaspoon sesame oil

FOR FORMING AND PAN FRYING

24 (3-inch) round dumpling, pot sticker or gyoza wrappers (found in the refrigerated aisle of your grocery store)
1 tablespoon peanut oil
1/3 cup warm water

Buffalo Chicken Wings

Devilishly spicy, super saucy and almost virtuous chicken in three steps.   Napkins anyone?

SERVES 4 AS A STARTER
OR 2 AS A MAIN COURSE

FOR THE WINGS

2 pounds bone-in, skin-on, chicken wing drummettes
2 tablespoons extra-virgin olive oil
sea salt and freshly ground black pepper

¼ cup melted butter
⅓ cup hot pepper sauce, such as Frank's Buffalo Sauce

minced garlic, chives or green onions, for garnish
celery sticks for serving

FOR THE BLUE CHEESE DIP

1½ cups crumbled blue cheese,
¼ cup low-fat buttermilk, plus more if needed
1 green onion, minced
sea salt and freshly ground black pepper, to taste

Preheat your oven to 400 degrees.

Line a large rimmed baking sheet with parchment paper.

MAKE THE WINGS: In a large bowl toss the chicken with the oil and ¼ teaspoon each of salt and pepper. Transfer chicken to prepared pan.   Roast without turning until golden and tender, about 30 to 40 minutes.

MAKE THE DIP: In a mini food processor, pulse together the blue cheese, buttermilk and green onion until desired consistency. Add more buttermilk and blend until smooth, if desired. Season with salt and pepper and set aside.

TO THE COOKED WINGS: In a large bowl, stir together hot sauce and melted butter. Add cooked chicken and toss to coat.

Sprinkle with the garnishes and serve them up!

Three-Cheese Mini-Macs
and Crispy Sesame Salad Stack

Three-Cheese Mini-Macs

Ah, macaroni and cheese-quite possibly the worlds best comfort food. If your only encounter with it has been by way of the blue box, this recipe could very well change your life, your lover's life, your friend's life and they will all love you forever! Oh! Never mind, I'm in Mac heaven!

**SERVES 6 AS A STARTER
OR 4 AS A MAIN COURSE**

FOR THE TOPPING

2 **slices good white bread (preferably sourdough), crusts removed, cut into ¼ to ½ inch pieces**
1 **cup sharp cheddar cheese, grated**
3 **tablespoons Parmigiano cheese, grated**
1 **teaspoon dried parsley or basil leaves**
2 **tablespoons butter, melted**

FOR MAC AND CHEESE

1 **cup elbow macaroni**
6 **tablespoons butter**
3 **tablespoons all-purpose flour**
2 **cups 2% milk**
½ **cup heavy cream**
2 **teaspoons ground mustard**
2 **teaspoons Worcestershire sauce**
¼ **teaspoon ground nutmeg**
¾ **teaspoon sea salt**
½ **teaspoon ground black pepper**
2 **cups sharp cheddar cheese (white, yellow or a mixture of both), grated**
½ **cup Fontina cheese, grated**
½ **cup Parmigiano cheese, grated**

Fill a large saucepan with water, salt it and bring to a boil. Add macaroni and cook for 2 minutes less than directed on package. Drain in a colander.

MAKE THE TOPPING: **Preheat your oven** to 375 degrees. Butter six 1-cup oven-proof baking dishes (or one 2 qt baking dish); set aside.

Place the bread, cheddar, Parmigiano and parsley in a medium bowl. Pour in 2 tablespoons melted butter and toss. Set the bread crumbs aside.

MAKE THE SAUCE: Melt butter in a large saucepan over medium heat. When butter bubbles, add the flour. Cook, stirring 1 minute. While whisking, slowly pour in milk and cream. Whisk until the mixture is thick and bubbly and coats the back of a spoon. Remove pan from heat. Stir in mustard, Worcestershire, nutmeg, salt, pepper and cheeses until smooth; set cheese sauce aside.

Stir cooked macaroni into the cheese sauce. Spoon mixture into prepared dishes. Sprinkle topping evenly over macaroni; bake until golden and bubbling 15 to 20 minutes.

Recipe hint

Fontina is a rich, semisoft cheese with a nutty flavor and faint sweetness, it marries well with the other cheeses in this mac and cheese.

Variation

Substitute panko bread crumbs for the bread slices. Approximately 2 cups.

Meaty Mains

Let these easy entrée recipes help you put dinner on the table when your energy levels are flagging. Pick from skillet suppers and other meaty offerings, all with minimal ingredients and maximum flavor.

Juneau

The "Capital City" is located on the Gastineau Channel in the panhandle of the state of Alaska and is the second largest city in the United States by area. The area of Juneau is larger than Rhode Island and Delaware individually and almost as large as the two states combined. Juneau is named after gold prospector Joe Juneau, though the place was for a time called Rockwell and then Harrisburg (after Juneau's co-prospector, Richard Harris).

The Taku River, just south of Juneau, was named after the cold t'aakh wind, which occasionally blows down from the mountains. Atop the surrounding mountains is the Juneau Icefield, a large ice mass from which about 30 glaciers flow; two of these, the Mendenhall Glacier and the Lemon Creek Glacier, are visible from the road system.

The Alaska State Capitol in downtown Juneau was originally built as the Federal and Territorial Building in 1931. Today, it is still the home of the state legislature and the offices of the governor and lieutenant governor.

Coffee Spice-Rubbed Spareribs

Sweet, savory and ohh so good. These are great to take to a summer picnic or to serve as a mid week dinner.

SERVES 6 AS A MAIN COURSE
OR 6 TO 10 AS A STARTER

FOR THE COFFEE-SPICE RUB

¼ cup firmly packed light brown
  sugar
2 tablespoons instant coffee
2 teaspoons unsweetened cocoa
  powder
2 teaspoons ground cumin
1 teaspoon chili powder
¼ teaspoon ground cinnamon
1½ teaspoons sea salt

FOR THE DIPPING SAUCE

¼ cup low-sodium soy sauce
2 tablespoons granulated sugar
2 tablespoons rice vinegar
1 teaspoon sesame oil
1 tablespoon fresh ginger,
  minced

FOR THE RIBS

2 full (13 rib) racks of pork spare
  ribs (about 2 lbs. each)

MAKE THE SPICE RUB: In a small bowl, combine all the seasoning ingredients.

MAKE THE DIPPING SAUCE: In a small saucepan over medium heat, bring all the sauce ingredients to a boil. Remove from heat and let cool.

MAKE THE RIBS: **Preheat your oven** to 325 degrees. Place the slabs on a baking sheet, liberally apply the rub on both sides and put them in the oven. After 1 hour, rotate the pan and check for doneness every 15 minutes. A skewer inserted between the ribs should meet little resistance. If the meat is still tough, keep cooking.

Remove from oven, put them on a cutting board meaty side down, let them rest for 10 minutes and slice them into individual ribs. Arrange the ribs on a platter and serve the sauce on the side.

Recipe hint

The membrane on the underside of the slab must be removed–it won't melt during cooking. Grab a corner of the membrane with a paper towel and pull it away from the bones. Trim off excess fat and pierce the ribs with a fork before applying the rub.

Variation

Tightly cover baking sheet with foil to seal in moisture and steam in the pan. Moist slow cooking keeps the ribs juicy and tender. If the meat has pulled away from the bones, your ready to grill.

My Tiny Alaskan Oven

Grilled Lamb Chops with Blueberry-Rosemary Sauce

If elegant is what you're after, lamb chops are the way to go. They make any dinner an occasion. Lamb chops are a sure sign of a fancy affair. But that doesn't mean they're hard to prepare or should be saved for special occasions. Actually, lamb chops can't be beat in the summer - they cook quickly and are perfect for grilling. If you've never purchased lamb chops before, it can get confusing. So here's what you need to know. There are two types of lamb chops available-rib and loin chops. If you're looking for the show-stopper with the long bone, buy rib chops. The loin chop is a tiny t-bone steak containing meat from both the tenderloin and the short loin. Be sure to let the lamb rest after its grilled. If it's sliced too soon, the juices will be lost, causing the meat to become dry.

MAKE THE SAUCE: In a small saucepan heat olive oil over medium heat. Add onion and garlic; cook and stir for 2 minutes until soft. Stir in remaining sauce ingredients. Bring to a boil; reduce heat and simmer uncovered, about 10 minutes or until desired consistency.

MAKE THE LAMB: Preheat grill or grill pan over medium-high heat; when hot, reduce to medium and coat with nonstick spray.

Brush lamb chops with sauce on one side and then grill in batches of 4 chops, glazed side down, 8 to 10 minutes per side for medium-rare. Glaze again, flip and grill the other side. Let chops rest 5 minutes before serving.

Serve with Blueberry-Rosemary sauce.

MAKES 8

FOR THE SAUCE

- 1 tablespoon extra-virgin olive oil
- ½ cup onion, chopped
- 2 cloves garlic, minced
- 1 cup blueberries
- ¼ cup ketchup
- 3 tablespoons sherry vinegar
- 2 tablespoons honey
- 1 tablespoon Dijon mustard
- 2 teaspoons fresh rosemary, minced
- 1 teaspoon hot chili sauce
- ¼ teaspoon sea salt

FOR THE LAMB

- 8 lamb rib or loin chops, trimmed, seasoned with sea salt and freshly ground black pepper

Chicken Pot Pie

A comfort-food classic, chicken pie is a wonderful one-dish meal. True, the crust takes time, but thanks to decent store-bought cooked chickens and broths, assembling the filling is as easy as pie.

SERVES 4

FOR THE PASTRY DOUGH

1½ cups all-purpose flour
1 teaspoon granulated sugar
¾ teaspoon sea salt
6 tablespoons cold butter, cubed
1 large egg yolk
2-3 tablespoons ice water

egg wash made by beating 1 egg
   with 1 Tbls. milk

FOR THE FILLING

4 tablespoons butter
1 cup onion, chopped
1 cup carrot, sliced ¼-inch thick
1 cup celery, sliced
1 cup button or cremini
   mushrooms, quartered
2 cups red potatoes, cubed
1½ teaspoons Old Bay seasoning
¼ teaspoon ground black pepper
½ cup all-purpose flour
⅓ cup sherry cooking wine
2 cups low-sodium organic chicken
   broth
1 cup half-and half
3 cups cooked shredded chicken
   (from 1 rotisserie chicken)
½ cup frozen peas, thawed
½ cup kernel corn, drained

Variation

Substitute one folded refrigerated unbaked pie crust for the pastry dough.

MAKE THE PASTRY: Place the flour, sugar, salt and butter in a food processor and combine for 15 seconds or until crumbly. Add the yolk and 2-3 tablespoons of water. Process in short bursts until the mixture just comes together. Add a little extra water if needed. Gather mixture together into a ball. Cover with plastic wrap and refrigerate for at least 15 minutes.

Preheat your oven to 350 degrees; line a baking sheet with foil.

MAKE FILLING WHILE DOUGH IS CHILLING: In a large saucepan, melt butter over medium heat. Add onions, carrots, celery, mushrooms and potatoes; stirring occasionally, until vegetables are just tender, 10 minutes. Stir in the seasoning, pepper and flour. Add the wine, scraping bits from the bottom of the pan.

Gradually add broth and half-and-half, stirring until mixture is smooth, then stir in chicken. Cook and stir until thick and bubbly, about 10-15 minutes. Off heat, stir in the peas and corn, season with ½ teaspoon salt and pepper; transfer filling to a 2½-quart baking dish.

Roll out prepared dough on a lightly floured surface to ¼-inch thick, then cut to fit the baking dish. Arrange dough on filling, trim and crimp edges. Make a small slit on top to allow the steam to escape. Transfer pot pie to the baking sheet. Brush dough with egg wash and bake pie until crust is golden, 35-40 minutes. Let stand 10 minutes before serving to set up.

Baked Pasta
with Béchamel Topping

This is a very common casserole found in the Greek cuisine and there are just as many versions of this recipe as there are casseroles in the U.S. Ground round can be substituted for the ground lamb if you choose. This is so simple and is my go-to recipe when company is coming!

Preheat your oven to 375 degrees.

MAKE THE MEAT LAYER: In a large nonstick saucepan over medium heat, add oil; when hot, add the onion and garlic and sauté until soft. Stir in the ground lamb and cook until crumbly and no longer pink; drain fat and discard. Pour in the water, wine and tomato sauce. Season with cinnamon, nutmeg, salt, pepper and cayenne. Cover and simmer stirring occasionally until thickened, about 15 minutes. Remove from heat.

MAKE THE PARMESAN CHEESE SAUCE: Melt butter in a medium saucepan over medium heat; whisk in flour. Pour in the milk, whisking until smooth. Whisk until the mixture is thick and bubbly and coats the back of a spoon. Stir in salt, nutmeg, cayenne and Parmesan cheese.

Add the lamb mixture to the cooked pasta and spread it into a 9 x 13-inch baking dish. Pour the cheese sauce evenly over the top of the pasta, smoothing to level. Sprinkle with nutmeg if desired. Bake until the top is golden brown, about 40 minutes. Remove from oven and let cool 15 minutes before serving.

Make ahead

This dish becomes even more flavorful each time it's reheated, making it the perfect make a day ahead of time dish. It can be assembled and placed in freezer. If frozen: Bring dish to room temperature and bake unthawed for 1 1/2 hours.

SERVES 6 TO 8

FOR THE PASTA

1 pound penne pasta, cook in a large pot of salted water until al dente, drain and put back in the pot

FOR THE MEAT LAYER

2 teaspoons extra-virgin olive oil
1 large onion, diced
6 large garlic cloves, minced
2 pounds ground lamb or lean ground round
1½ cups water
½ cup sherry cooking wine
1 (16-ounce) can tomato sauce
1 teaspoon ground cinnamon
½ teaspoon ground nutmeg
1 teaspoon sea salt
½ teaspoon ground black pepper
¼ teaspoon ground cayenne

FOR THE PARMESAN CHEESE SAUCE

½ cup (1 stick) butter
½ cup all-purpose flour
3 cups 2% milk
¾ teaspoon sea salt
¼ teaspoon ground nutmeg
⅛ teaspoon ground cayenne
1 cup Parmesan cheese, grated

Seining

Gillnetting

Charter Fishing

Hoisin-Glazed Meatloaf

When served with a side of mashed potatoes (or mac and cheese), meatloaf is the perfect comfort food. Here, try a new take on the classic meatloaf, with two intriguing variations on the theme: A fancy version that is just right for meatloaf sandwiches and Hoisin-glazed minis that are perfect for a party.

MAKES 1 MEATLOAF
OR 12 MINI MEAT LOAVES

FOR THE HOISIN-GLAZE

1 (8-ounce) jar Hoisin sauce
½ cup rice vinegar
1 1-inch piece ginger, peeled, minced
2 garlic cloves, minced

FOR THE MEATLOAF

2 slices white bread or bread on hand, cut into ½-inch cubes
½ cup reduced-sodium organic chicken broth
2 tablespoons butter
6 cloves garlic, minced
1 3-inch piece ginger, peeled, minced
1 medium carrot, grated
1 medium onion, diced
2 stalks celery, diced
2 pounds lean ground round
1 pound ground Italian sausage or unseasoned ground pork
2 eggs
1 teaspoon Chinese five-spice powder
1¼ teaspoons sea salt
1 teaspoon ground black pepper
2 tablespoons of the reserved glaze

MAKE THE HOISIN-GLAZE: In a medium saucepan over medium heat, bring all ingredients to a boil. Reduce heat to low and simmer, stirring often, until sauce thickens to a glaze, about 10 minutes. Let cool.

MAKE THE MEATLOAF: **Preheat your oven** to 375 degrees. In a large bowl, soak bread cubes in chicken broth, until liquid is absorbed. Heat butter in a large skillet over medium-high heat. Add garlic, ginger, carrot, onion and celery. Cook for 5 minutes and set aside to cool.

To the bread mixture add meat, eggs, spice, salt, pepper and 2 tablespoons of the cooled glaze. Add the cooled vegetables. Using hands, mix well until combined. Turn meatloaf into a rimmed baking sheet lined with parchment paper, shape into a loaf. Make shallow indentations around the sides. Using a pastry brush, generously brush the glaze over the loaf, **reserving some to serve with**. Bake for 1 hour or until internal temperature reaches 155°F. Let meatloaf cool, 10 minutes before slicing.

Variation

Spray a 12-cup muffin pan with nonstick cooking spray. Divide meat mixture among prepared muffin cups; brush tops of meat loaves with the glaze, **reserving some to serve with**. Place the muffin pan on a rimmed baking sheet lined with parchment paper to catch the drippings. Bake for 30 to 45 minutes or until internal temperature reaches 155°F. Carefully remove from cups immediately and place on rack to cool.

Pan-Roasted Rib Eyes

This chili sauce and steak are a match made in heaven, but this sauce has a few other divine uses. Try it spooned over pork chops or spread it over roasted fish.

MAKE THE SAUCE: Place a small saucepan over medium heat. When hot add the oil. When oil is hot add the garlic and sauté about a minute. Immediately stir in the broth, cream, soy sauce, lemon juice, chili sauce and cornstarch. Stir until thickened; stir in basil.

MAKE THE RIB EYES: **Preheat your oven** to 400 degrees. Season steaks generously with salt and pepper. Scatter thyme and rosemary sprigs evenly in bottom of a rimmed roasting pan; dot with 4 tablespoons butter.

Melt 1 tablespoon butter with 1 tablespoon oil in a large heavy skillet over medium-high heat. Reduce heat to medium and add two steaks to the skillet. Cook until seared and golden brown on all sides. Transfer steaks to prepared roasting pan. Repeat with remaining 1 tablespoon butter, 1 tablespoon oil and steaks.

Roast steaks in oven, turning halfway through cooking and basting frequently with herb butter in pan, about 10 to 15 minutes or to desired doneness.

Transfer to warm plates. Drizzle 1 tablespoon herb butter from roasting pan over each steak. Spoon the sauce over the rib eyes, sprinkle on the cheese and walnuts and serve at once.

Note

This recipe easily doubles.

SERVES 4

FOR THE SAUCE

1 tablespoon peanut oil
2 cloves garlic, minced
⅔ cup low-sodium organic chicken broth
⅓ cup heavy cream
2 tablespoons low-sodium soy sauce
2 tablespoons lemon juice
1 teaspoon hot chili sauce
1 teaspoon cornstarch
2 tablespoons fresh basil, chopped

FOR THE RIB EYES

4 (1-inch thick) bone-in rib eyes
sea salt and freshly ground black pepper
10 fresh thyme sprigs
5 fresh rosemary sprigs
6 tablespoons butter, divided
2 tablespoons extra-virgin olive oil, divided

¼ cup blue cheese, crumbled
¼ cup walnuts, toasted

Caramelized Chicken with Apples

This is such a fabulous way to cook chicken and so simple. It's quick enough for a midweek meal and fancy enough to serve to special company.

SERVES 4

- 4 chicken breasts, skinless and boneless
- ⅓ cup all-purpose flour
- ½ teaspoon sea salt
- ¼ teaspoon ground black pepper
- ¼ cup butter
- 3 apples, peeled, cored and cut into ½-inch slices
- 1 tablespoon lemon juice
- 3 tablespoons maple syrup or pancake syrup

Place chicken between two pieces of plastic wrap; with flat side of meat mallet, pound to flatten chicken to ½-inch thick.

Place flour on a small plate, add salt and pepper. Dip chicken in flour, shaking off excess. Melt butter in a large nonstick skillet over medium heat. Add chicken; cook 5 to 6 minutes or until no longer pink, turning once. Place on platter; cover loosely with foil.

Add the apples to the same skillet, cook 2 to 3 minutes without stirring or until lightly caramelized. Stir apples, cook 1 more minute. Stir in the lemon juice. Add the maple syrup, stirring to combine. Serve sauce and apples over chicken.

Roasted Cauliflower

- 1 medium head cauliflower
- 2 tablespoons extra-virgin olive oil
- ¼ teaspoon sea salt

Preheat your oven to 400 degrees. Toss cauliflower with oil and salt in a large bowl. Spread in 1 layer on a large rimmed baking sheet and roast, stirring and turning occasionally, until tender and golden brown, 25-30 minutes.

Roasted Honey and Lemon-Glazed Chicken

In an uncertain world, we all need a truly excellent recipe for roasted chicken, one that will never fail. Here it is. Yes, basting is well worth the effort-it gives the chicken a beautiful burnish.

Preheat your oven to 450 degrees.

In a small bowl, whisk together the honey, lemon juice and soy sauce. Set the chicken in a cast-iron skillet (or ovenproof skillet) and tuck the wing tips underneath. Sprinkle the cavity with ½ teaspoon salt and stuff with rosemary, garlic and lemon wedges. Brush half of the honey glaze over the chicken and season with remaining salt.

Roast for 30 minutes. Reduce the oven temperature to 325 degrees. Rotate the chicken and brush with remaining glaze. Tent with foil; continue cooking until an instant-read thermometer inserted into the thigh (avoiding bone) registers 165°F. and juices run clear, about 45 minutes.

Transfer the chicken to a carving board and let rest 10 minutes before carving. Pour pan juices into a glass measuring cup; skim fat from the top. Strain, and serve sauce with chicken, if desired.

Recipe hint

Cooking two birds at once provides dinner plus leftovers for the days ahead.

SERVES 4

- 1 **whole roasted chicken (about 4 lbs.)**
- ¼ **cup honey**
- 2 **tablespoons lemon juice**
- 2 **tablespoons low-sodium soy sauce**
- 1 **teaspoon sea salt, divided**
- 3 **large fresh rosemary sprigs**
- 3 **large garlic cloves, quartered**
- ½ **lemon, cut into 4 wedges**

There is no need to convince the thousands of Alaskans and avid outdoorsmen and women, who get excited by reeling in a 30-pound king salmon or seeing a beautiful coho rise to a brightly colored lure, why in the springtime they need to start making plans to head outside. But for some reason, after a long winter off I always need a little convincing. As a new salmon season approaches, I try to remember all the reasons why I love to fish. Because surely it's not all the sleepless nights, the isolation and all the aches and pains it causes.

As I try to remember, I've compiled a list of 10 good reasons that just might offer you an excuse to call in sick for the summer and go fishing.

1. Freedom: Ask most fishermen why they enjoy spending time on the water and you're likely to hear the word "freedom." Spending a summer fishing helps to release us from our highly stressful, everyday environment. Nothing brings on the sense of being alive and aware to help rebuild our personal reserves like a day spent with nature. You are aware of each minute, what is happening right now and what is ahead. You're free in that you've just done something all day long and then you are done... When you wake up, you're on the water and in one of the most beautiful places on earth.

2. Not Ruled by the Clock: Having a bad day of fishing still beats a day in the office or tending to house chores. When fishing, your day is ruled by the tide. Watching the sun rise and set is a pretty neat way to keep track of time. You're not on a clock; you're run by the wind, waves and tide. In this way, you develop confidence in yourself and in your ability to handle unexpected situations.

3. The Thrill: Fishing has a way of fulfilling an age-old need of pursuing and catching. The thrill lies in the challenges, such as finding where the fish are and keeping your boat afloat. But, there are many who will be quick to profess that it's not in the catching of fish that's important, but in the immeasurable life lessons that you will experience along the way. This gives me joy because when I am fishing, my entire spirit is elevated and this makes me happy.

4. Health Benefits: More than fifty percent of Americans are over weight. Being outside and being active helps to make you feel better and encourages a healthier way of life. Driving to your local grocery store and fast food restaurant might be convenient, but fishing can also help you burn those unwanted calories, increase the quality of your lifestyle and add years to your life.

5. Physical and Mental Strength: Mental strength sometimes can be more important than physical strength. The summer gives you the opportunity to sharpen both. No doubt fishing is exercise. Every single muscle works on a boat. Even when you are just sitting at anchor your body is working as the boat rocks and rolls. Plus, your getting lots of fresh air and plenty of sunshine. Fishing really comes down to mental toughness and being physically strong to make it to the end.

6. Fishing for Food: Wild fish are low in fat and cholesterol and high in protein. In fact, the American Heart Association recommends a regular diet of fish. Besides it's a lot more challenging to catch a plate of fresh fish than stroll endlessly down a supermarket aisle. We dine on fresh fish 5-7 days a week and love every minute of it. Eating this much fresh fish is the perfect opportunity to lighten up my diet and loose a few extra pounds.

7. Boost to the Economy: The fishing industry is Alaska's largest private employer and employs over 65,000 people for the summer, seasonal and year round employment. The state fisheries average over $11.2 billion in revenue per year and account for 38% of the dollar value landed in the United States. This gives an economic boost that any state government would be pleased with. I love being a part of this.

8. Self Fulfillment: Fishing offers you the chance to improve your self-esteem through respect for the environment, mastering outdoor skills and achieving personal goals. Every day is filled with opportunities to learn something new or sharpen a skill such as, tying knots, piloting the boat, chart reading, how to anchor, how to make meals onboard with ease and how to read the wind, tide and weather.

9. Empowerment: There is nothing better than coming back to town after a season, knowing you have pushed yourself to the limits way beyond what most people could only imagine and you had an experience of a lifetime.

10. Lifestyle: The industry, the people, the lifestyle. It's all a part of who I am. It isn't worry free, luxurious or comfortable at times. But it's perfect for me. At the end of every season I walk away with a better understanding of who I am and tons of great stories to tell for years to come. After all fishing in Alaska is an adventure of a lifetime. I love the lifestyle it provides. We fish for 15 weeks a year and get to do what we want to do for the winter which is traveling, taking beautiful photos and writing cookbooks. ✂

LaDonna

Baked Pork Chops Stuffed with Apricots and Leeks

These thick pork chops are bursting with stuffing. The mixture of sweet, salty, smoky and savory sensations pump up the flavor and keeps the chops moist as they bake. When choosing pork chops to stuff, look for ones that are about 1½-inches thick.

SERVES 4

FOR THE STUFFING

½ cup dried apricots, chopped
2 quality thick-cut bacon slices, chopped
½ cup leeks, chopped
¼ cup celery, chopped
1 cup cubed dried bread
1 egg, beaten
½ teaspoon dried thyme
⅛ teaspoon ground cinnamon
¼ teaspoon sea salt
¼ teaspoon freshly ground black pepper

FOR THE PORK CHOPS

4 bone in center- cut rib pork chops (1½-inches thick)

1 teaspoon dried thyme
½ teaspoon sea salt
½ teaspoon freshly ground black pepper
2 tablespoons extra-virgin olive oil

MAKE THE STUFFING: Place apricots in a small bowl of hot water. Let stand 10 minutes; drain.

Cook the bacon in a medium skillet over medium heat until it just begins to brown. Add leeks and celery; cook until vegetables are soft. Place vegetables in a small bowl and stir in all remaining stuffing ingredients. Refrigerate until chilled.

MAKE THE PORK CHOPS: **Preheat your oven** to 350 degrees. With a small sharp knife, cut a pocket inside of each chop cutting to the bone. Stuff each chop with one-fourth of the stuffing.

In a small bowl, stir together 1 teaspoon thyme, ½ teaspoon salt and ½ teaspoon pepper; press onto both sides of chops. Heat oil in a large skillet over medium-high heat until hot. Add chops, in batches if necessary; cook, turning once, 6 to 8 minutes or until browned on both sides.

Place chops on a rimmed baking sheet; bake 15 to 20 minutes or until stuffing is hot and chops are pale pink in the center. Place chops on a platter and cover loosely with foil. Let stand 7 to 10 minutes before serving.

Parmesan-Crusted Pork Chops

Using thin pork chops ensures the meat will just finish cooking when the Parmesan crust turns golden brown. Squeezing lemon wedges over the chops cuts some of the richness from the crust. For a quick-to-fix accompaniment, serve a salad of baby greens or arugula lightly dressed with extra-virgin olive oil and lemon juice.

In a small shallow bowl, stir together bread crumbs, cheese, oregano, salt and pepper. Place flour in another shallow bowl; place beaten eggs in a third shallow bowl.

Dip each chop in flour, shaking off any excess. Dip in egg, dip in bread crumb mixture, patting both sides to make sure mixture adheres well.

Heat 2 tablespoons of the oil in a large skillet over medium-high heat until hot. Add half of the chops, cook 3-5 minutes or until golden brown, turning once. Keep warm in a 250 degree oven while cooking remaining chops. Serve with lemon wedges.

SERVES 4

2 cups panko bread crumbs
½ cup Parmesan cheese, grated
1 tablespoon fresh oregano, chopped
1 teaspoon sea salt
½ teaspoon freshly ground black pepper
¼ cup all-purpose flour
2 eggs, beaten
8 boneless thin-cut pork loin chops
4 tablespoons extra-virgin olive oil, divided
lemon wedges

Tarragon-Cream Chicken

Got a package of chicken breasts and a half an hour? Then you're well on your way to a great-tasting dinner.

4 chicken breast, boneless, skinless
freshly ground black pepper
¼ cup all-purpose flour
2 tablespoons extra-virgin olive oil
1½ cups white mushrooms, halve
   if large
3 ounces prosciutto, sliced (if you
   don't have prosciutto, use bacon
   and drain well, or just omit it)
1 cup dry white wine or low-sodium
   chicken broth
1 cup heavy cream
2 teaspoons fresh tarragon
1 teaspoon apple cider vinegar
fresh chives or green onions, minced

Rosemary Buttered Noodles

8 ounces dried egg noodles.
4 tablespoons butter
2 teaspoon fresh rosemary,
   minced
Parmesan cheese, grated
freshly ground black pepper

Season chicken with pepper. Dust each breast with flour, shaking off any excess. In a sauté pan, sauté chicken in olive oil over medium-high heat. Cook until lightly browned on both sides, 5-7 minutes. Remove chicken, set aside and keep warm. Add mushrooms and prosciutto to the pan. Cook until mushrooms soften and begin to brown, 2-3 minutes. Add wine (or broth) and heavy cream. Return chicken to the pan, reduce heat and simmer until sauce thickens slightly, about 8 minutes. Stir in tarragon and vinegar; cook 1 minute. Garnish with chives. Serve with buttered noodles.

MAKE THE BUTTERED NOODLES: Cook noodles as directed on the package. Drain, but do not rinse. Melt butter over medium heat in the same pan that was used to cook the noodles. Add the rosemary and cook until fragrant, about 1 minute. Add drained noodles to the pan and toss to coat with the butter, then transfer to a serving dish. Top noodles with Parmesan cheese and black pepper.

Flank Steak with Peppers and Onions

There is something about the flavors of coffee and beef that go together so well. A little bit of brown sugar in the spice mixture adds the perfect amount of sweetness.

MAKE THE SPICE RUB: Combine 2 tablespoons brown sugar, the instant coffee, cocoa powder, ground cumin, chili powder, cinnamon and salt in a bowl. Generously rub steak with the coffee spice mixture.

Heat oil in a large skillet over medium-high heat until hot. Add steak, in batches if necessary and reduce heat to medium; cook, turning once, 3 to 4 minutes per side for medium-rare. Transfer to cutting board; cover loosely with foil. Let rest 5 minutes, then thinly slice the steak across the grain. Reserve the juices in the skillet.

Add the remaining 1 teaspoon brown sugar and the onion to the skillet. Sprinkle with ¼ teaspoon salt and pepper to taste; cook over medium-high heat, stirring frequently, until the onion is soft and golden. Add the bell peppers and ¼ cup water; cook, stirring until crisp tender, about 5 minutes. Stir in the lime juice.

Divide the steak, bell peppers, onion and the juices from the skillet among plates. Serve with lime wedges.

Recipe hint

Flank steaks yield juicy results when quickly cooked to medium-rare or medium; cooking longer can make the meat tough.

Variation

Feel free to get creative with the uses for this spice rub. T-bone steak, ribs, venison, chicken and salmon are fantastic. This rub is also great for quick-cooking fajitas.

SERVES 4

FOR THE SPICE RUB

2 tablespoons plus 1 teaspoon brown sugar
1 tablespoon instant coffee
1 teaspoon unsweetened cocoa powder
1 teaspoon ground cumin
½ teaspoon chili powder
⅛ teaspoon ground cinnamon
1 teaspoon sea salt

1 to 1½ pounds flank steak, cut into 2-3 pieces
2 tablespoons extra-virgin olive oil, divided
1 large onion, cut into wedges
sea salt and freshly ground black pepper
1 red, green and yellow bell pepper, cut into strips
juice of ½ lime, plus lime wedges for serving

Seafood Mains

We catch most of our food right off the back of our boat. As you might imagine, we eat lots of salmon, which is one of the best foods on the planet. I'm talking about wild salmon, not farmed salmon. Without grabbing my megaphone and climbing up on my soap box, I do need to say this. We have a saying here in Alaska: "Friends don't let friends eat farmed salmon!" Many salient health reasons exist, which a quick Google search will relay (including some of my own passionate crusading).

Haines

Haines was named in honor of Francina Haines of the Presbyterian Home Missions Board. Accompanied by his friend John Muir (a naturalist), S. Hall Young, was the first missionary to the area in 1879. The purpose of their trip was to scout a location for a mission and a school.

The first known meeting between white men and the Tlingit took place in 1741 when a Russian ship anchored near Haines and started a fur trade in the area. In 1892, Jack Dalton established a toll road on the Tlingit trade route into the Interior to cash in on gold-seekers and others heading north into Canada. Parts of the Dalton Trail are now the Haines Highway.

In November, Haines hosts the annual Bald Eagle Festival. Starting in September through early December, Haines welcomes over 3,500 bald eagles to the beautiful Chilkat River Valley. Spectators from around the world come to partake in this fascinating migratory event. Haines is also home to the Discovery Channel's hit show "Gold Rush Alaska." This reality show has put gold fever back into the American mind set and has now been signed for a second season.

Haines is like no other destination. With fascinating history, intriguing culture, breathtaking scenery and adventure to last a lifetime, there's no question that your time spent in Haines will be enjoyed and remembered for years to come.

Crab Imperial with Red Pepper

Being an Alaskan fisherwoman I have had my share of crab imperial. I have also experimented with making them. I love this recipe because you can taste the crab. Ole calls this dish crab pudding and requests it all the time. It's creamy, decadent and will be enjoyed by the entire family.

SERVES 4-6

½ cup (1 stick) butter, divided
　　(melt 3 Tbls. for topping)
3 tablespoons all-purpose flour
2 cups heavy cream
1 cup panko bread crumbs, divided
½ cup red bell pepper, diced
¼ cup onion, finely diced
4 tablespoons fresh parsley, minced
　　and divided
2 tablespoons sherry cooking wine
2 tablespoons lemon juice
1 tablespoon grated lemon zest
1½ teaspoons Worcestershire
　　sauce
1 teaspoon paprika, divided
1 teaspoon ground mustard
½ teaspoon hot chili sauce
2 cups fresh Dungeness crabmeat
　　(about 2 crab, cooked and cleaned)
¾ teaspoon sea salt
¼ teaspoon ground black pepper
toasted baguette slices, for
　　serving

Preheat your oven to 375 degrees.

In a large nonstick saucepan over medium heat, melt 5 tablespoons butter. Whisk in the flour. While whisking, slowly pour in the cream.

Whisk until the mixture is thick and bubbly and coats the back of a spoon. Remove from heat and stir in ½ cup of the bread crumbs, the bell pepper, onion, 2 tablespoons parsley, wine, lemon juice, zest, Worcestershire, ½ teaspoon paprika, mustard, chili sauce and crabmeat. Season with salt and pepper.

Divide mixture evenly among six 6-ounce oven-proof baking dishes (or four 1-cup); place on a rimmed baking sheet and set aside.

In a small bowl, mix remaining 3 tablespoons melted butter, ½ cup bread crumbs, ½ teaspoon paprika and ½ teaspoon parsley. Sprinkle evenly over each baking dish. Bake until lightly browned and bubbling in the center, about 20 minutes. Serve hot with baguette toasts.

Sautéed Snapper with Fresh Avocado Salsa

A few thoughts before you get started on the salsa. Make sure the tomatoes you use for this dish are nice and hard, with no hint of ripening. Look for avocados that are ripe but still firm–the ones on which the stem at the end still wiggles. And finally, this salsa can be made up to a day ahead, though the fresher it is, the brighter it will be.

SERVES 4

FOR THE SALSA

2 medium tomatoes, seeded and diced
1 avocado, pit removed and diced
juice of ½ lime
3 green onions, sliced
½ cup kernel corn, drained
¼ cup fresh basil leaves, minced
2 tablespoons extra-virgin olive oil
2 garlic cloves, minced
1 teaspoon honey
¼ teaspoon ground cumin
sea salt and freshly ground black pepper

FOR THE SNAPPER

4 (6-ounce) snapper fillets, skin and pin bones removed
1 tablespoon butter
1 tablespoon extra-virgin olive oil
sea salt and freshly ground black pepper
fresh basil, minced

MAKE THE SALSA: Gently combine the diced tomatoes and the remaining salsa ingredients in a medium bowl, folding with a wooden spoon to prevent breaking the avocados; season to taste.

MAKE THE SNAPPER: Rinse the fillets carefully, pat dry with paper towels. Season the fish on both sides with salt and pepper. Heat a large nonstick skillet over medium-high heat. Add the butter and oil. Place the fish in a single layer in the pan. Cook 3 minutes on each side or until fish flakes easily when tested with a fork. Serve immediately with a generous serving of salsa and a sprinkling of basil.

Variation

Substitute cod, flounder or halibut.

Dungeness Crab Soft Tacos

These are so much fun. How about a taco party? You can set everything out on the table and let your guests build their own tacos. Or you can serve them all assembled if you prefer. Cooked shrimp could easily replace the crab to make this dish more elegant.

In a large bowl; gently combine crabmeat through black pepper.

When you are ready to serve, heat the tortillas in a dry skillet until just warm and softened, keeping them under a kitchen towel as you go. Place the tortillas on plates, spoon on a layer of the mixture and sprinkle with a little crumbled cheese. The way to eat these is to fold the taco in half and eat by hand; it can get messy, so have plenty of napkins ready to go!

SERVES 4

2 cups fresh Dungeness crabmeat
   (about 2 crabs, cooked and cleaned)
2 medium tomatoes, seeded and
   diced
1 avocado, pit removed and diced
⅓ cup green onions, sliced
4 garlic cloves, minced
1 jalapeño pepper, seeded, minced
¼ cup fresh basil leaves, chopped
¼ cup fresh cilantro, chopped
⅓ cup lime juice
¼ teaspoon sea salt
¼ teaspoon freshly ground black
   pepper

8 stone-ground corn tortillas
2 cups feta cheese, crumbled

Dungeness Crab Cantonese

This is the kind of over-the-top meal guests will talk about for days afterward and it's simple to prepare. Crab, ground pork and a host of Asian condiments create delicious mouth-watering flavors.

Stir together cornstarch, broth, rice wine, soy sauce, sugar, ginger and pepper in a small bowl until sugar is dissolved, set aside.

Heat the oil in a large skillet or wok over medium-high heat. Add the garlic and pork and stir-fry until pork is no longer pink. Stir in the cornstarch mixture and bring to a boil. Add the crabmeat, reduce heat and simmer until thickened. Stir in the chopped green onions.

Pour the eggs over the crab, stirring gently until the egg is just set. Drizzle with the sesame oil and serve over hot cooked rice.

Recipe hint

Pasteurized crabmeat comes in three forms: lump, backfin or claw. All work as fine substitutes in this recipe—but pick through the meat for bits of shell.

Simple Steamed Rice

Bring 2½ cups water to a boil in a medium saucepan. Stir in 1 cup long-grain white rice and ½ teaspoon salt. Return to a boil over medium-high heat. Reduce heat and simmer covered until rice is tender and has absorbed all the water. 16-18 minutes. The rice will be studded with steam holes when ready. Remove from heat and let stand covered for 10 minutes. Fluff with a fork before serving.

MAKES 4 SERVINGS

- 2 tablespoons cornstarch
- 2 cups reduced-sodium organic chicken broth
- ¼ cup rice wine
- 2 tablespoons low-sodium soy sauce
- 1 teaspoon granulated sugar
- 1 teaspoon fresh ginger, minced
- ¼ teaspoon ground black pepper
- 1 tablespoon extra-virgin olive oil
- 2 large garlic cloves, minced
- ½ pound unseasoned ground pork
- 2 cups fresh Dungeness crabmeat (about 2 crab, cooked and cleaned)
- 4 green onions, chopped
- 2 eggs, slightly beaten
- 1 teaspoon sesame oil
- hot cooked jasmine rice

Sweet and Savory

1 tablespoon butter
2 teaspoons minced garlic
2 teaspoons grated fresh ginger
1 jalapeño pepper, seeded and minced
1 (18-ounce) jar orange marmalade
3 tablespoons lime juice
1 tablespoon whole-grain mustard
1 teaspoon prepared horseradish
¼ teaspoon sea salt

In a medium saucepan, melt butter over medium-high heat. Add garlic, ginger and jalapeño pepper; Cook for 2 minutes, stirring constantly. Reduce heat to medium-low. Add marmalade, lime juice, mustard, horseradish and salt. Simmer for 5 minutes, stirring frequently. Serve warm.

Tartar Sauce

2 cups mayonnaise
⅓ cup celery, minced
⅓ cup onion, minced
2 tablespoons lemon juice
1 tablespoon Worcestershire
   sauce
pinch sea salt
pinch ground mustard
pinch ground black pepper
2 tablespoons dill pickle relish

Combine all ingredients and mix well.

Clarified Garlic Butter

Clarifying butter removes the water and milk solids, leaving pure butterfat. Clarified butter can stand being cooked longer and at a higher temperature. It will keep for 3 to 6 months in the refrigerator or freezer.

2 sticks butter
2 cloves garlic, minced

Cut butter into pieces and melt slowly in a heavy saucepan over low heat. Simmer gently until foam rises to the top of the melted butter. Remove from heat and skim foam from the surface with a spoon. Pour clarified butter over garlic, into a bowl leaving milky sediment behind. Serve warm.

Dungeness Crab
with Three Dipping Sauces

Crab: to Boil or to Steam? If you've never cooked live crabs, it can seem intimidating. Here are two methods for getting the critters in the water. Bring a large pot of salted water to a vigorous boil over high heat. Toss in 1 or 2 crabs and boil for 25 minutes. On the other hand... steam them. Add water about 2 inches up the side of a deep pot, then suspend a strainer over the water. Place 1 or 2 crabs in the strainer, depending on its size. Cover the pot tightly and steam over high heat for 25 minutes. The crab will be filled, not with water, but with delicious undiluted juices. Make sure to have seafood crackers or small hammers on hand to get at all of the sweet, flaky meat. If you find yourself with left over crabmeat, use it in Crab Croquettes, Crab Stuffed Mushrooms or Dungeness Crab Soft Tacos.

Lemon-Pepper Silver Salmon

It doesn't get simpler than this. To round out your Sunday supper, serve this dish with Baked Acorn Squash with Brown Sugar.

Preheat your oven to 400 degrees.

Set the fillet on a rimmed baking sheet lined with parchment paper. Rub the fillet with the olive oil. Sprinkle with the lemon-pepper mixture. Gently rub the seasoning into the fillet.

Bake 15-20 minutes or until fish flakes easily when tested with a fork.

SERVES 4

- 1½ **pounds skin-on salmon fillet, pin bones removed**
- 1 **tablespoon extra-virgin olive oil**
- ⅛ **teaspoon sea salt**
- ¼ **teaspoon freshly ground black pepper**
- ½ **teaspoon granulated sugar**
- 2 **teaspoons grated lemon zest**
- 1½ **teaspoons fresh thyme, chopped**

Baked Acorn Squash with Brown Sugar

- 2 **medium acorn squash, halved crosswise. Scoop out seeds; discard. Slice a small piece off bottom of each to level.**
- 4 **tablespoons butter**
- 4 **tablespoons light brown sugar**
- **sea salt**
- **freshly ground black pepper**

Preheat your oven to 425 degrees. Generously butter a rimmed baking sheet. Set squash halves, scooped sides down, on prepared sheet. Bake until golden, 20-25 minutes. Turn squash, prick insides all over with a fork. Divide butter and brown sugar among halves. Season with salt and pepper. Continue to bake until flesh is easily pierced with the tip of a pairing knife, 20 minutes. Serve warm.

> **Did you know?** Black bears spend six to eight months a year feeding heavily in preparation for the lean winter months. In spring they feed on a wide variety of green vegetation, such as grasses and sedges. In summer and fall, bears with access to salmon streams gorge on fish. Berries such as huckleberry, currant, blueberry, devil's club and others, provide a critical carbohydrate boost. Throughout summer, bears will dig up marmots, till meadows for roots and tear apart logs for insects.
>
> Bears tend to be solitary animals except females with cubs. Bear cubs are born mid-winter, tiny and blind and nurse through the winter sharing their mother's fat reserves through her rich milk. A female will typically have two or three cubs and they will stay with her until heading out on their own as two-year-olds. Mother bears are fiercely protective of their cubs.
>
> The best time to watch for bears is in the spring and summer during the dawn and dusk hours when they are actively searching for food. The shoreline is a common place to see bears beach-combing for dead animals, foraging for shellfish or grazing on sedges. In late July through early September, look for them at streams feeding on spawning salmon.

Pan-Grilled Halibut with Hoisin Glaze

For me, halibut is one of the finest eating sea fish there is as long as it's not over cooked. It's delicate, flaky white meat is one of the most sought after here in Alaska. If you're fortunate enough to find some of this fresh delicacy, don't bother with the fancy cookbooks, here's a simple surefire way to prepare it that will give you the tastiest and easiest dinner ever.

SERVES 4

2 tablespoons orange juice, divided
4 (6-ounce) halibut fillets, skinned and trimmed
sea salt
freshly ground black pepper
2 tablespoons hoisin sauce
¼ teaspoon hot chili sauce
cooking spray

Preheat a grill or stovetop grill pan to medium-high heat. Brush 1 tablespoon orange juice evenly over fillets; sprinkle evenly with salt and pepper. Combined hoisin sauce, chili sauce and remaining 1 tablespoon orange juice in a small bowl.

Coat the grill pan with nonstick cooking spray. Place fillets on the pan and brush with hoisin mixture. Cook 3 minutes on each side or until fish flakes easily when tested with a fork; brushing occasionally with hoisin mixture.

Recipe hint

Thoroughly cooked fish are opaque and have milky juices. Poke them with a fork at the thickest part of the fillet to see if they begin to flake easily. Fish that are translucent, with clear juices, are not fully cooked.

Hazelnut-Crusted Halibut with Apple Salsa

If you've read my other books, you know how much I love making salsas. They're easy to do, easy to eat and leftovers are great for a midnight snack. They are quick, making them perfect for entertaining.

Preheat your oven to 400 degrees. Line a rimmed baking sheet with parchment paper.

MAKE THE CRUST: Whirl ingredients in a mini food processor until nuts are finely chopped. Place nuts on a plate.

MAKE THE HALIBUT: Brush halibut with melted butter and pat hazelnut mixture all over. Place on the prepared baking sheet. Bake 15-20 minutes or until fish flakes easily when tested with a fork.

MAKE THE SALSA: Warm the oil in a medium sauté pan over medium-low heat. Add shallots and apple and cook until slightly softened, about 3-4 minutes. Remove from heat. In a small bowl, whisk together lemon juice and remaining ingredients; stir into apple mixture. Serve halibut with the apple salsa.

Variation

Cut the halibut into 4-inch slices to use for halibut tostadas or halibut tacos.

SERVES 4

FOR THE HAZELNUT CRUST

¾ cup dry roasted hazelnuts
⅛ teaspoon ground mustard
½ teaspoon sea salt
¼ teaspoon ground cayenne
1 tablespoon grated lemon zest
1 teaspoon thyme leaves

FOR THE FISH AND SALSA

4 (6-ounce) halibut fillets, skinned
   and trimmed
3 tablespoons butter, melted
3 tablespoons extra-virgin olive oil
2 tablespoons shallots or green
   onions, minced
2 apples, cored and cut into
   ½-inch dice
2 tablespoons lemon juice
2 teaspoons Dijon mustard
½ teaspoon thyme leaves
¼ teaspoon sea salt
¼ teaspoon freshly ground pepper
pinch of ground cayenne

Ketchikan airport ferry

Artichoke Onion Pasta with Jumbo Prawns

Not everyone has the luxury of buying really fresh (off the boat) shrimp. If fresh is not available to you, buy frozen as most "fresh" shrimp in the grocery stores is thawed-out frozen shrimp. Thawed shrimp has a shelf-life of only a couple of days versus frozen shrimp which retains its quality for several weeks. Defrost shrimp in the refrigerator or in cold water. Shrimp cooks very quickly, so defrosting in the sink or microwave is a big no-no. While we're on the topic, I'm a big believer in consuming sustainable foods (whenever location, pockets and circumstances allow it) and this includes seafood. The Monterey Bay Aquarium has a guide to purchasing sustainable seafood, including shrimp, on its website. Please visit and see how you can help our oceans and sea life thrive.

In a large sauté pan over medium heat, cook the onion and garlic in reserved artichoke liquid until tender. Add the artichoke hearts, tomatoes and oregano, simmer for 5 minutes.

Add prepared pesto and salt and heat for one additional minute.

Transfer pasta to a warm serving platter. Pour sauce over and toss just to blend. Arrange prawns on top.

Garnish with Parmesan cheese and serve.

Note

Shhhh! Don't tell Ole I forgot to put the prawns on the pasta before he took the photo.

Easy Steamed Shrimp

Into a steamer pot add 1-inch water, bring to a boil on medium heat. Then place the steam basket with the shrimp into the pot. Place a lid on the pot and steam for about 10 minutes. (Start timing once the water is boiling). Allow steam to cook shrimp, until shrimp have changed color to light pink.

SERVES 4

- 12 ounces bow tie pasta, cook al dente, drain and set aside
- 1 pound "cooked" large shrimp, peeled, leaving tails intact
- 1 large onion, chopped
- 4 large garlic cloves, minced
- 1 (7-ounce) jar marinated artichoke hearts, halved (reserve 3 tablespoons of liquid
- 1 (15-ounce) can diced tomatoes
- 1 cup cherry tomatoes, halved
- 1 teaspoon dried oregano
- ½ cup prepared pesto
- ¼ teaspoon sea salt
- ¾ cup Parmesan cheese, grated

Bacon-Wrapped Halibut

One of the benefits of living in Southeast Alaska is the availability of a diverse range of fresh seafood. It makes experimenting a bit more challenging and puts my creative brain to the test. It was time for me to think of something different. And then, I found my star ingredient. Bacon! The halibut turns out flaky and full of bacon juice. These make you feel as if you should add bacon to your dinner every night!

SERVES 4

- 4 (6-ounce) halibut fillets, skinned and trimmed
- 2 teaspoons Old Bay seasoning
- 2 teaspoons fresh dill, minced
- 4 slices quality thick-cut bacon
- 4 teaspoons extra-virgin olive oil
- 1 lemon, cut into wedges

Carmelized-Onion Mashed Potatoes

- 2 teaspoons extra-virgin olive oil
- 1 medium onion, chopped
- 1½ pounds baking potatoes, peeled and chopped
- ½ cup low-fat buttermilk
- 2 tablespoons butter
- ¼ teaspoon sea salt
- ¼ teaspoon freshly ground black pepper

Heat a skillet over medium-high heat. Add olive oil to pan; swirl to coat. Add onion, sauté a few minutes or until golden. Set aside.

Place potatoes in a saucepan. Cover with water, bring to a boil. Reduce heat and simmer until tender; drain. Stir in buttermilk, butter, salt and pepper; mash with a potato masher. Stir in reserved onion.

Season the halibut with the Old Bay seasoning and dill. Wrap the bacon tightly around the middle of the fillet.

In a large nonstick skillet, heat 1 teaspoon oil over medium-high heat. Add the fish, secured side down and cook turning once until the bacon is crisp, about 8 minutes. Serve immediately with lemon wedges.

Recipe hint

The meat of halibut is white, mild flavor and comes in steaks and fillets. Although it's a firm fish, it's a tad bit delicate. So be careful when turning it.

Variations

Halibut BLT's are absolutely yummy with this recipe. Or, cut the halibut meat into manageable chunks, then wrap a strip of bacon around the fish and stick it onto a skewer. Put the skewers on the grill. I try to make sure the bacon-covered edge is on the grill so the halibut will not flake. Depending on your grilling style, time will vary, but I cook them until the bacon is cooked.

Honey-Garlic Shrimp

Nothing beats the clock like stir fry cooking. If you plan on serving this dish with rice, start the rice first. While it's cooking, cut up the vegetables and make the stir fry.

In a small bowl, stir together soy sauce, honey and garlic.

In a wok or large skillet, heat oil over medium-high heat until hot. Add carrots and zucchini. Cook 2 minutes, stirring constantly or until vegetables are slightly tender; remove vegetables from wok. Add shrimp.

Cook and stir 2 minutes or until shrimp just begin to turn pink. Return vegetables to wok, stir in soy sauce mixture. Cook, stirring occasionally, 2 minutes or until shrimp turn pink and liquid has thickened slightly. Serve with hot cooked jasmine rice, if desired

SERVES 4

¼ cup low-sodium soy sauce
2 tablespoons honey
2 garlic cloves, minced

1 tablespoon peanut or olive oil
2 cups carrot, julienned
2 cups zucchini, julienned
1 pound "uncooked" medium shrimp, peeled, leaving tails intact

Did you know? Killer whales, also known as Orcas, are not really a whale at all but are members of the dolphin family. They are called killer whales because they are great hunters. Males can be as much as 30 feet long and weigh up to 20,000 pounds while still being able to swim at a top speed of 30 miles an hour. They are social animals and live in family-related groups known as pods. Pods may have up to 40 members, made up of both males and females. To sleep they take catnaps on the surface of the water. During the summer months, from June to September, the northern resident whales can generally be seen from northern Vancouver Island to Alaska.

My first salmon on a rod during the filming of "Hookin' Up" with Mariko Izumi

Garlic-Coconut Sockeye Salmon

This simple crowd pleaser recipe is wonderful for fresh salmon fillets or steaks (you can use previously frozen salmon as well). It can be made up in minutes and is a delightful mingling of sweet and savory, making it perfect for an everyday meal or for your next barbecue party or cookout.

SERVES 4

FOR THE SALMON

4 (6-ounce) wild salmon fillets, skin and pin bones removed
1 teaspoon sesame oil
2 tablespoons extra-virgin olive oil
¼ cup low-sodium soy sauce
1 tablespoon honey
2 teaspoons garlic, minced
2 teaspoons fresh ginger, peeled, minced
1 tablespoon rice vinegar
1 cup green onions, chopped

FOR THE GARLIC-COCONUT

1 tablespoon extra-virgin olive oil
¼ cup flaked coconut
1 tablespoon garlic, minced
sea salt

MAKE THE SALMON: In a medium bowl, whisk together the sesame oil, olive oil, soy sauce, honey, garlic, ginger, vinegar and half of the green onions. Place salmon fillets in a shallow baking dish (or zip top plastic bag) and pour half the marinade over them. Refrigerate 30 minutes, turning once.

MAKE THE GARLIC-COCONUT: In a small sauté pan over medium heat, add oil and coconut. Cook, stirring until coconut is golden. Add the garlic and cook 1 minute. Remove from heat and season with salt.

MEANWHILE: In a small saucepan, heat remaining marinade mixture to a syrupy glaze, 2-3 minutes; remove from heat and set aside.

Preheat grill or stovetop grill pan to medium-high heat. Remove salmon from marinade and pat dry. Brush salmon with additional olive oil and grill 3 minutes skinned-side up. Turn and brush with reserved glaze. Continue grilling 3-5 minutes or until fish flakes easily when tested with a fork. Transfer salmon to a platter and brush with any additional glaze. Lightly press the reserved garlic-coconut on the top of each salmon fillet. Garnish with remaining green onions and serve.

Soy-Glazed Black Cod with Orange Zest

In the deep blue depths of Alaska's pristine waters lies what some would consider the best tasting fish in the world–Black Cod. This incredibly flavorful fish is also referred to as Sablefish or Butterfish. It is widely known as an excellent fish for gourmet entrées and well received when smoked. Its name, Butterfish, is thought to be derived from the fact that it has a soft, buttery, delicate texture. Prepared correctly, it will literally melt in your mouth. This is by far the best recipe I have for Black Cod and will definitely be a keeper for you!

Combine half of the green onions, soy sauce, sugar, rice wine and orange zest in a zip-top-bag. Add the fish and marinate 45 minutes to one hour in the refrigerator, turning occasionally.

Preheat your oven to 400 degrees. Place remaining green onions in a shallow baking dish, lay the fillets over the top. Toss marinade. Bake for 15 minutes or until fish flakes easily when tested with a fork.

Serve with Jasmine rice and and Lemon Broccolini.

Checking for doneness

To check whether your fish is cooked: Insert a fork into the thickest part of the steak or fillet and gently pull the meat apart. If the inner flesh is still translucent and dense (not flaky), the fish still requires a few more minutes of cooking time. When done, the inner flesh will be opaque and will flake easily. And remember, fish continues to cook after it's been removed from the heat.

SERVES 4

8 green onions, chopped and divided
½ cup low-sodium soy sauce
6 tablespoons granulated sugar
¼ cup rice wine or white wine
1 tablespoon grated orange zest
4 (6-ounce) black cod fillets

Lemon Broccolini

2 teaspoons extra-virgin olive oil
2 (6-ounce) bunches Broccolini
¼ teaspoon sea salt
¼ teaspoon freshly ground black pepper
1 teaspoon grated lemon zest

Heat oil in a large skillet. Add Broccolini, salt and pepper; sauté 5 minutes or until crisp-tender. Remove from heat, stir in lemon zest.

Fun facts about Alaska

- Average salmon boat is 37 ft. long.
- 50% of U.S. Seafood production is produced in Alaska.
- State Fish: King salmon (Oncorhynchus tshawytscha).
- King salmon weighing up to 100 lbs. have been caught in Alaska.
- State Marine Mammal: Bowhead whale.
- State Sport: Dog Mushing.
- Alaska is the only state to have coastlines on three different seas: Arctic Ocean, Pacific Ocean and Bering Sea.
- Alaska has 34,000 miles of coastline.
- Alaska has 3 million lakes.
- Alaska has 29 volcanoes.
- Alaska is home to North America's tallest peak, Mount McKinley (known to the locals as Denali) which is 20,320-feet tall located in the Alaska Range.
- Barrow, Alaska is the most northerly community in the U.S.
- The name of Alaska comes from the Aleut word Alyeska, meaning The Great Land.
- Alaska nicknames include The Last Frontier, Land of the Midnight Sun.
- The Alaska state flag was designed by Benny Benson at age 13.
- Juneau, Alaska is the only capital in the United States accessible only by boat or plane.
- The US purchased Alaska from Russia in 1867 for $7,200,000 (about 2 cents an acre) and made it the union's 49th state on January 3, 1959.
- Alaska is the largest state in the union, covering 570,373 square miles, approximately one fifth of the entire United States. Alaska is so large that it is twice the size of Texas and the state of Rhode Island could fit into Alaska 425 times.
- The population of Alaska is only 626,932 and compared to the population of bears in Alaska, there is 1 bear for every 21 people.
- There are more active glaciers and ice fields in Alaska than in the rest of the inhabited world.
- The largest glacier is Malaspina at 805 square miles.
- The Arctic Circle is an imaginary circle around the globe where on December 21 the sun never rises for twenty-four hours and on June 21 for twenty-four hours it never sets.
- Giant vegetables are common in Alaska due to the extremely long days in summer. Alaska has grown a record cabbage weighing in at 94 pounds.

–courtesy of Alaska Seafood Marketing Institute

Misty Fjords is a pristine masterpiece featuring some of Alaska's most spectacular scenery. Seventeen thousand years ago the area was covered in ice. Massive glacier action carved out its present landscape. Misty Fjords road-less location is only accessible by float-plane or boat from Ketchikan.

Halibut in Parchment

Cooking fish encased in parchment or foil is a wonderful way to get the best results and add a dramatic flair to dinner. The paper or foil holds in the moisture, concentrates the flavor and protects the delicate flesh. The fish essentially steams in the oven and in its own juices. Follow the folding and cooking instructions carefully. The "foil" packets can be cooked in the oven or on the grill.

Preheat your oven to 400 degrees.

Cut four pieces of parchment (doubled over) which is large enough to encase your filet with an inch or so margin around it. I like cutting a heart shape for the packet - remember grade school Valentines?

Divide zucchini among one-side of the heart in thin layers. Sprinkle garlic and sliced basil over, dividing equally. Scatter tomato halves around zucchini. Drizzle each packet with 1 tablespoon wine and ½ tablespoon oil. Place a fish fillet atop each portion. Season with salt and pepper, drizzle ½ tablespoon olive oil over each.

Beginning at the wider part of the Valentine, began folding the paper over itself. As you move around the paper, you'll end up at the pointed end of the heart, fold under. Place packets in a single layer on a large rimmed baking sheet. Bake until fish is just cooked through (a toothpick poked through the parchment will slide through fish easily) approximately 15 to 20 minutes.

Carefully cut open packets (steam will escape). Garnish with basil leaves.

Variations

Substitute salmon, cod, or any of your favorite fish fillets. Add carrots, celery, mushrooms or any of your favorite vegetables.

SERVES 4

- 2 medium sized zucchini, thinly sliced
- ¼ cup garlic, thinly sliced
- ¼ cup fresh basil, thinly sliced, plus more for garnishing
- 24 cherry tomatoes, halved
- 4 tablespoons sherry cooking wine
- 4 tablespoons olive oil, divided
- sea salt and freshly ground black pepper
- 4 (6-ounce) halibut fillets, skinned and trimmed

Seared Salmon with Green Bean-Radish Salad

This dish is so-o-o delicious and so-o-o simple to make! Perfect for a hot summer's day.

SERVES 4

2 tablespoons balsamic vinegar
2 tablespoons shallot, minced
¼ cup plus 1Tbls. extra-virgin olive oil, divided
sea salt
ground black pepper
4 (6-ounce) wild salmon fillets, skin and pin bones removed
½ pound green beans, trimmed or asparagus
1 cup cherry tomatoes, quartered
4 radishes, thinly sliced

In a medium bowl, whisk together vinegar, shallot and ¼ cup oil; season to taste with salt and pepper. Set aside. In a pan of boiling water, cook the green beans until crisp tender, about 4 minutes.

Season salmon with salt and pepper. In a large nonstick skillet, heat remaining 1 Tbls. oil over medium-high heat; add salmon skinned-side up and cook 2-3 minutes each side or until fish flakes easily when tested with a fork. Arrange green beans on 4 plates. Top each with a salmon fillet. Spoon vinaigrette over salmon; scatter tomatoes and radishes on top and serve.

Rosemary and Garlic Roasted Salmon

Pungent rosemary is one of my favorite herbs. Incredibly versatile, it's pine-like flavor complements everything from meat to vegetables to fish. Rosemary can easily tolerate heat from cooking, but use it sparingly. Its strong flavor can quickly take over a dish.

SERVES 4

2 tablespoons extra-virgin olive oil
sea salt
freshly ground black pepper
2 sprigs rosemary, (about 2 Tbls.)
   strip the needles from the stems
   and finely chop
3-4 cloves garlic, minced
4 (6-ounce) wild salmon fillets, pin
   bones removed (substitute cod or
   halibut)

Preheat your oven to 400 degrees.

Place salmon fillets skin side down on a parchment lined baking sheet.

Evenly distribute olive oil on each salmon fillet. Sprinkle salt and pepper over the fillets. Next, add the rosemary and garlic and lightly press into the salmon.

Bake for 15-20 minutes or until fish flakes easily when tested with a fork. Serve and enjoy!

Calico Beans

One of our all-time favorite side dishes with fish is Calico Beans. It's quick, simple and oh so good!

SERVES 4-6

½ pound lean ground beef
½ pound good-quality bacon,
   cut up
1 medium onion, chopped
1 (15-oz.) can Northern beans, drained
1 (15-oz) can Pork & beans
1 (15-oz) can Chili beans
½ cup ketchup
1 teaspoon sea salt
2 tablespoons cider vinegar
¾ cup light brown sugar
1 tablespoon yellow mustard

Preheat your oven to 350 degrees. In a large skillet over medium-high heat; cook the beef, bacon and onion until browned. Transfer to a large oven proof baking dish. Add remaining ingredients. Bake covered for 1½ hours. Or in a crock pot for 3 hours.

Crab Cakes with Cucumber Dipping Sauce

I just love crab cakes and I love dipping sauces, too. So that's why this dish would have to go on my top ten favorites. I know it's Ole's favorite dish. I should dedicate this recipe to him. I think I will.

MAKE THE CRAB CAKES: In a large bowl; combine all ingredients, (except sesame seeds and oil) stirring gently to combine. Dividing evenly, form mixture into 8 to 10 cakes. Dredge each mound in panko and sesame seeds to coat, set aside.

In a large nonstick skillet over medium-high heat; sauté half the cakes in 1½ tablespoons of oil. Cook until golden, about 3 minutes, then carefully flip the cakes over and cook on the other side about 2 minutes more. Transfer to a paper-towel-lined plate. Sauté remaining cakes in the same manner.

MAKE THE DIPPING SAUCE: Bring the water to a boil and add the sugar and salt, stirring to dissolve. Remove from heat and add the vinegar, red pepper flakes, shallot and cucumber. Stir to mix the ingredients and refrigerate until ready to use.

Serve 2 cakes per plate along with a small dish of cucumber dipping sauce and a tossed green salad. Garnish each plate with a cilantro sprig.

MAKES 8-10 CAKES

FOR THE CRAB CAKES

4 cups fresh Dungeness crabmeat (about 4 crab, cooked and cleaned)
½ cup mayonnaise
½ cup fresh parsley, chopped
4 cloves garlic, minced
¼ cup lemon juice
1 large egg
2 teaspoons Dijon mustard
1 tablespoon Old Bay seasoning
1 cup panko bread crumbs, plus ½ to ¾ cup for forming

⅛ cup sesame seeds
olive oil or peanut oil for frying

FOR THE DIPPING SAUCE

1 cup water
¼ cup granulated sugar
1 teaspoon sea salt
¼ cup white vinegar
pinch of red pepper flakes, or as needed
1 large shallot, peeled and finely minced
½ English cucumber, peeled, cut in half lengthwise, seeded and cut into ¼-inch slices

cilantro sprigs for garnish
lemon wedges for serving

I love working along side my husband. And I love the Alaskan lifestyle. It isn't worry free, luxurious or comfortable at times. But it's perfect for me.

SERVES 4

4 (6-ounce) wild salmon fillets, skin
   and pin bones removed
¼ cup light brown sugar
1 teaspoon sea salt
1 teaspoon ground black pepper

FOR THE GLAZE

¼ cup cherry preserves
¼ cup ketchup
⅛ cup chipotle chiles in adobo
½ teaspoon fresh thyme
¼ teaspoon ground cumin
juice of ½ lime
salt to taste
1½ tablespoons extra-virgin olive oil

JALAPEÑO-LIME BUTTER

½ cup (1 stick) salted butter, room
   temperature
1 tablespoon fresh cilantro, minced
1 tablespoon jalapeño, seeded,
   minced
juice of ½ lime

Combine all ingredients in a small bowl using a rubber spatula. Roll flavored butter in plastic wrap and chill until firm.

MANGO-APPLE SALAD

1 mango, peeled, diced
1 Granny Smith apple, diced
juice of 1 lime
fresh cilantro, chopped, optional

Combine and set aside.

Rub salmon fillets with brown sugar, salt and pepper and place on a baking sheet lined with parchment paper. Cover and chill for 30-60 minutes.

MAKE THE GLAZE: In a food processor or blender, purée the preserves, ketchup, chiles, seasonings, lime juice and oil until smooth. Set aside.

Pat the fillets dry with paper towels. Spread about a tablespoon of glaze over each fillet and marinate for 15 minutes (reserve the remaining glaze for serving). Preheat grill or stovetop grill pan to medium-high; oil the grates lightly when hot. Wipe off some of the glaze and grill skinned side up at a 45˚ angle to grates. Cook 3-5 minutes, turn fillets and grill until fish is just cooked through, about 3 or 4 minutes more. Serve the salmon with Jalapeño-Lime Butter, reserved glaze, Mango-Apple Salad and Sesame Rice Cakes.

Sesame Rice Cakes

These are fun to make and serve along side your main dish.

MAKES 8 CAKES

3 cups "cooked" jasmine rice, cooled to room
   temperature (or cold)
1 tablespoon granulated sugar
1 tablespoon rice vinegar
1 tablespoon cornstarch
1 tablespoon sea salt
¼ cup sesame seeds
2-4 tablespoons extra-virgin olive oil

Combine rice, sugar, vinegar, cornstarch and salt. Scoop and press rice into a ¼-cup measuring cup coated with nonstick cooking spray. Tap cake out onto a parchment-paper lined baking sheet. Gently press sesame seeds on the tops of each cake. Heat 2 Tbls. oil in a large skillet over medium-high heat. Add rice cakes, seed side down and sauté 5 minutes on each side or until rice is golden. Add additional oil as needed to prevent burning.

Grilled Salmon with Cherry-Chipotle Glaze

Most of the time, "dressing up" foods with fancy preparations and sauces just mask flavors. But curing fresh salmon with sugar and salt, then grilling it in a sweet-spicy glaze really enhances an already great tasting fish. The chipotle chili glaze has some kick, but the cherry preserves in it helps tone down the "fire." And it doesn't stop there! Cilantro-Lime Butter finishes the dish easily—and with style.

Seared Halibut with a Tangy Marmalade Glaze

A colorful blend of orange, avocado, hazelnuts and dried cranberries gives the dish a bright and vibrant flavor. Serve it on a bed of protein-rich quinoa or couscous for extra nutritional value.

SERVES 4

- 1 avocado, pit removed
- 1 (8-ounce) can mandarin oranges, drained
- 4 (6-ounce) halibut fillets, skinned and trimmed
- sea salt
- freshly ground black pepper
- 1 tablespoon extra-virgin olive oil
- 2 tablespoons orange marmalade
- Hot cooked quinoa or couscous
- ¼ cup dried cranberries
- ⅓ cup hazelnuts, toasted and chopped

Cut avocado into ¼-inch cubes and set aside. Rinse halibut and pat dry. Sprinkle lightly with salt and pepper.

Pour oil into a large nonstick frying pan over medium-high heat. When hot, add halibut and cook, turning once, until opaque but still moist looking at the center of the thickest part, about 6 minutes total. Spread marmalade evenly over each piece of fish.

Mound couscous on dinner plates. Place a piece of fish on top of couscous and arrange avocado and orange segments over the fish. Sprinkle evenly with cranberries and hazelnuts.

Did you know? In the first months of 1926, Territorial Governor George Parks was working hard for the cause of statehood. During a trip to Washington, D.C., he saw the flags of the 48 states flying outside the old Post Office Building and after conversing with the postmaster general he was convinced that Alaska also needed a flag to fly alongside the others. He persuaded the Alaska American Legion to hold a contest open to all Alaskan children grades 7-12 to design a flag for the state. The contest winner was Benny Benson, a seventh grader at the territorial school at Seward. His design of eight stars to represent the Big Dipper placed on a blue background to represent the sky, was a unanimous winner by a panel of judges. The North Star is for the future of the state of Alaska, the most northerly of the Union.

Sweet Treats

Craving something sweet but aren't keen on spending lots of time in the kitchen? Try any of our cookies, confections and other stylish treats that satisfy with little effort.

Skagway

The city is located in the Upper Lynn Canal and is considered the northernmost point in Southeast Alaska. It's 80 air miles from the capital city of Juneau and 110 road miles from Whitehorse, Yukon Territory, Canada.

The Port of Skagway is the northernmost ice-free, deep-water port in North America and serves as a year round transportation hub between Alaska, Northern British Columbia and the Northwest Territories.

As of the 2010 census, the population of the city was 920. However, the population doubles in the summer tourist season for the 900,000 plus visitors.

The White Pass and Yukon Route narrow gauge railroad, part of the area's mining past, is in operation purely for the tourist trade and runs throughout the summer months.

Skagway is also part of the setting for Jack London's book "The Call of the Wild" and for Joe Haldeman's novel "Guardian."

Cream Puffs with Coffee Ice Cream

Sometimes a recipe is so very exquisite, so very delicious, that you just have to cook it for friends. This is that sort of recipe.

SERVES 8
THREE PUFFS EACH

FOR THE PUFFS

1 quart coffee ice cream
½ cup (1 stick) unsalted butter, cut
   into pieces, plus more for
   baking sheets
1 cup water
¼ teaspoon sea salt
1 cup all-purpose flour
4 large eggs, lightly beaten

FOR THE CHOCOLATE SAUCE

½ cup granulated sugar
1 cup heavy cream
7 ounces 60%-cocoa bittersweet
   chocolate, finely chopped
½ teaspoon vanilla extract

MAKE THE CHOCOLATE SAUCE:

Heat sugar in a 2-quart saucepan over medium heat, stirring with a fork to heat sugar evenly, until it starts to melt, swirling pan occasionally so sugar melts and is dark amber. Remove from heat, add cream and a pinch of salt. Return to medium-low heat and cook until caramel has dissolved. Remove from heat and add chocolate, whisking until melted; whisk in vanilla. Keep warm.

MAKE THE CREAM PUFFS: Chill a small metal baking pan in the freezer. Form 24 ice cream balls (2-3 tablespoons each) and freeze at least 1 hour (this will make assembling it faster).

Preheat your oven to 425 degrees with racks in upper and lower thirds. Line two large rimmed baking sheets with parchment paper.

Bring butter, water and salt to a boil in a 2-quart heavy saucepan, stirring until butter is melted. Reduce heat to medium, add flour and cook, beating with a wooden spoon, until mixture pulls away from the sides of pan and forms a ball, about 30 seconds. Remove from heat and cool 1 minute. Add eggs 1 at a time, beating well with an electric mixer after each addition. Drop heaping tablespoons of batter onto baking sheets (you should have 24-28), about 2-inches apart. Bake, rotating sheets between racks halfway through, until puffed and brown, about 20-25 minutes. Remove from oven; **(turn off oven)**. Prick each puff once with a skewer, then return to oven to dry, with door propped open, for 10 minutes.

FILL THE PUFFS: When cool, halve each puff horizontally, then fill each with a ball of ice cream. Arrange 3 filled puffs on each plate and drizzle generously with warm chocolate sauce. Serve immediately.

Recipe hint

The ice cream balls can be frozen up to a day. The puffs can be baked 1 day ahead and cooled completely, then kept in an airtight container. The chocolate sauce is perfect for chocolate covered strawberries.

Place butter in a stainless steel bowl. Set aside. In a heavy saucepan, whisk together the milk, egg yolks, sugar, cornstarch, vanilla and salt and cook over medium-high heat, whisking constantly, until the mixture becomes very thick and begins to boil. Place a sieve over the bowl of butter and press the custard through the sieve. Stir to incorporate. Cover the mixture with parchment paper pressed directly on the surface and refrigerate. When the custard is cool, whip the heavy cream until stiff. Fold half of the whipped cream into the custard, then fold in the remaining whipped cream. Fill each puff with the custard-whipped cream mixture. Dust with confectioners' sugar.

Alternative Cream Filling

2 tablespoons butter
2 cups whole milk
4 egg yolks
½ cup granulated sugar
¼ cup cornstarch
1 teaspoon vanilla extract
⅛ teaspoon sea salt
1 cup heavy cream
confectioners' sugar

Rhubarb and Strawberry Shortcakes

"Simple" is such a lovely word and so appropriate for fresh rhubarb and strawberries, which are at their flavorful best when paired with home-made shortcakes and gingered whipped cream.

MAKE THE COMPOTE: Combine the rhubarb, sugar, orange juice, honey, all the cardamom, salt and vanilla in a heavy 3-quart saucepan. Bring to a simmer over medium-low heat, stirring often. Simmer until the rhubarb releases its juice and becomes tender, 5 minutes. Add the strawberries and simmer until they start to soften and the rhubarb breaks down slightly, 1 to 3 minutes. Pour the mixture into a bowl. Cool to room temperature, stirring occasionally. Add more sugar and orange juice, if needed.

MAKE THE SHORTCAKES: Preheat your oven to 425 degrees.

Stir the dry ingredients into a large mixing bowl. Add vanilla to the cream and mix into the flour with a wooden spoon. Add more cream as necessary until the dry ingredients become a firm ball of dough with no dry spots. It should not be sticky. Turn the dough onto a lightly floured surface and knead about 20 times, until the dough becomes smooth. Pat into a 9-inch square.

Using a 3-inch round cookie cutter, cut 8 rounds of dough. Brush each shortcake on both sides with melted butter and place on a parchment-paper lined baking sheet. Place in the oven and bake until puffed and lightly golden, about 15 minutes. Place shortcakes on a wire rack to cool. Tease the shortcakes apart with a fork. Divide the rhubarb mixture among the shortcakes and finish with a dollop of whipped cream.

MAKES 8 SHORTCAKES

STRAWBERRY-RHUBARB COMPOTE

- 4 cups fresh rhubarb ½-inch thick sliced
- ½ cup granulated sugar, plus more as needed
- 6 tablespoons orange juice, plus more as needed
- 3 tablespoons honey
- ¼ teaspoon plus ⅛ teaspoon ground cardamom
- ¼ teaspoon sea salt
- 1 teaspoon vanilla extract
- 3 cups hulled and thickly sliced strawberries (about 2 pints)

FOR THE SHORTCAKES

- 2 cups all-purpose flour
- ¼ teaspoon sea salt
- 1 tablespoon baking powder
- 1 tablespoon granulated sugar
- 1 teaspoon vanilla extract
- 1¼ cups heavy cream, plus more as needed
- 2 tablespoons melted butter

GINGERED WHIPPED CREAM

- 1 cup heavy cream
- 2 teaspoons granulated sugar
- ½ cup candied ginger, diced
  Whip on medium-high speed until soft peaks form. Gently stir in candied ginger.

Speaking of Sweet...

Keta the Sea Cat

EVERY FISHING BOAT should have a sea cat and I am the Sea Cat on the *LaDonna Rose*. The first thing you should know about me is that my Dad never fails to remind me that being THE SEA CAT is not the equivalent of being THE CAPTAIN of the *LaDonna Rose*. I beg to differ with him but that is a story for another day.

Ole and LaDonna found me when they were in Florence, Oregon and visited the Florence Humane Society, which was then my temporary home. I saw them when they first came into my temporary quarters and thought to myself, "now that looks like a nice couple, maybe they will adopt me." I am not one to take chances, so as soon as they came into the room, I jumped up onto a ledge, went over to Dad, stood up on my hind legs and put my head on his shoulder. The first thing I noticed, once I got up close, was that he smelled a little bit like fish. Home Run I thought to myself. Here is a nice couple that loves the same thing I crave regularly for dinner.

I consider myself to be beautiful, since I have a loving face, a long bushy tail, a sleek velvet-like blackened golden coat and golden soft eyes. In addition, I am full of personality, funny, fun to be around and curious to a fault. Mom and Dad scooped me out and I just knew if I could get them to pick me up I would be home free. Fortunately for me, Dad made the first move and bent down and picked me up. I purred like crazy and rubbed against him until Mom took me away from Dad and started talking to me in baby talk. Yes, I was just a kitten, but baby talk, come on, give a lady a break. In the end, my antics were successful and before they left they adopted me and took me away. Shortly thereafter, I had my first scary experience and began to seriously wonder if I had made a big mistake. They took me onto what they referred to as an airplane and off we went to some faraway place they called Ketchikan, Alaska. It was my first time flying and I have to admit I was more than a bit frightened at first but once the big bird got off the ground without crashing I relaxed and had a nice flight. As soon as we arrived in Ketchikan I experienced my second period of misgiving about my future. Mom and Dad took me out and put me on a boat docked in a place called Refuge Cove. It was just sitting there silently floating in the water. The first thought that came to mind was "Don't these people know cats love fish but HATE water." What in the world is wrong with them, haven't they ever had a feline child?

Initially, I staggered around on the boat on my stubby legs and fell over or ran into everything on board. Once I had snooped around for a while, I decided being on a boat might not be too bad, at least until I walked over and looked over the side and saw the water, which I knew was deep and COLD. I quickly decided anything would be better than my digs at the Humane Society so I decided right then and there to make the best of my situation and began to scamper about the boat looking at all the equipment and sticking my nose into whatever I could find.

I had wondered from the moment Mom and Dad adopted me what they would name me but they had not even discussed it until after we came on board. Soon the issue of my name came to the forefront and Dad wanted to call me "Raccoo" since he thought I looked like a raccoon. Can you believe, he thought beautiful feline me looked like a dumb raccoon? First, raccoons like water and I hate water and the only thing I can think of we have in common is we will both eat fish. Fortunately, Mom thought it was a bad idea too and said to Dad: "Raccoo is no name for a cat, have you ever heard of a cat named Raccoo?" Go for it Mom, let him have it. Mom suggested that if Dad was going to name me Raccoo he might as well name me "Keta," a salmon named after a dog. Although it was blatantly obvious to everyone that I am neither a fish nor a dog, Dad clearly thought Mom's facetious suggestion was a great idea (dumb but great?) and so I was named for a fish. Disgusting, NO? Mom and Dad let me spend my first few days on the boat exploring on my own which was great fun and educational to boot. Since I had never been on a boat, there was a lot of new stuff to explore, rub against and sniff.

It wasn't long before I demonstrated my jumping skills and hopped up onto the cooler. Once on the cooler I had to strain my neck to look up and see the flying bridge that towered into the sky. I then went about inspecting all the ropes, buoys and lines lying all over the place and soon came up on a ladder that led up to the flying bridge. Since I had not perfected my skills at climbing ladders I quickly looked for and found an alternative way to get to the bridge. There was a stand that held the net drum in place that was closer to the flying bridge. Since cats are very agile, along with a lot of other very positive characteristics, I made a strong leap up and onto the stand and confidently jumped up to the bridge. I discovered the bridge was full of interesting things like fishing poles, a life ring and Mom and Dad's survival suits. I also spotted what looked to me like the galley stove pipe and boy was I surprised when I walked over and discovered it was nice and warm. Immediately, I knew where I was going to hide out when I was not able to get into the cabin on a cold day. You have no idea how many times I have returned to my personal little heater box to warm myself and take a well-earned and needed nap.

Once I had finished a cursory inspection of the flying bridge I began looking for a way down. Descending on a rope did not particularly appeal to me and I was then no better at walking down a ladder than I was at walking up the ladder. I tried meowing to see if Mom or Dad would come, pick me up and put me on the deck, but alas I had no success whatsoever. Therefore, on a whim and fancy, I simply jumped the 5 or so feet from the flying bridge down to the deck, did a nice kitty role (it would have gotten at least a 9.5 at the Olympics) and proudly stood up. No applause please by the audience. I looked around and it was obvious Mom and Dad had witnessed my miraculous feat and that they knew, or at least assumed, that their new Sea Cat was having a great time and was going to love and enjoy her new home.

All the effort of checking out the boat was making me hungry and all of a sudden I smelled something good. I immediately headed for the galley and when I jumped down into the galley I found myself face-to-face with what had all the appearances of a hot tiny oven. Mom was standing there by the oven doing some cooking and I knew in my heart that, if I would cuddle up and make her my "best" friend she would give me something special to eat.

I knew something new was going to happen in my life when Dad started the engine and Mom and Dad begin to pull in the lines and buoys. However, I never imagined the boat was movable and that I would be taken away from the dock. Slowly, the boat moved away from the dock, which made me very nervous, and as I looked up I could see the masts of other boats as we passed one another. My first thought was "Now, where are they taking me and what new adventure am I going to be forced to endure." It was a warm sunny day and since I had no idea where we were going I decided I would find a nice warm spot on the dash in front of Dad in the cabin and lie down. Soon boredom took over and so I jumped down from the dash and ran out onto the deck. I found a nice sunny spot by the railing where I could watch all that was going on around me. The water was full of wales, porpoises, seals, sea lions and even a school of leaping fish. Just watching the fish jump made me hungry and I began praying one of them would make a mistake and land on the deck so I could try eating fresh fish for the very first time. We spent many hours moving across the water and when Dad announced we had reached the fishing grounds, Mom and Dad set out the net and began fishing in earnest. There was not anything for me to do on the deck and with Mom working I knew I was not about to be fed. Thus, I thought it would be appropriate to demonstrate to Mom and Dad my innate feline intelligence and I slowly, but carefully, climbed the ladder up to the flying bridge. Once I got onto the bridge, I had the perfect spot to sit and watch what was taking place on the deck below. It was not long before Mom and Dad began to pull in the net and pretty soon there were silver fish flying and flopping all over the deck. It was exciting to see and all I could think of was getting down on the deck and playing with the fish. I was afraid I would take a bad tumble if I tried climbing down the ladder so I started meowing loudly and hoped that Mom or Dad would hear me and come and get me and put me down.

I was less than successful in getting their attention, and so once again I was forced to jump from the flying bridge to the deck. Once I was down on the deck, I carefully approached the flapping fish and when the opportunity arose I would swat one with my paw. Mom and Dad were so busy pulling in the net and removing the fish that they did not see their new Sea Cat in her first real fishing experience. Bummer.

I continued to paw at and play with the fish and played let's pretend. I imagine myself to be a fisherman pulling in a large fish from the sea; or, as a brave sailor braving the storm while riding on the back of a humpback whale. Now how is that for a feline imagination? I was just getting comfortable with all the flipping and flopping fish around me when a a strange bird landed nearby and began to squawk incessantly. It definitely got my attention and I began wondering if I could catch it and have some lunch. I crouched down close to the deck and began to slowly approach the bird. Then, all of a sudden, the bird saw me and begin acting like it was going to attack me. One thing I am not, and that is a fool, so I immediately hightailed it out of there and headed for a safe and secure place to hide.

Later in the afternoon after Mom and Dad had pulled in the net and put all the fish in the hold, Mom began cooking dinner in the tiny oven in the galley. The smell of freshly cooked salmon was soon in the air and I was famished from all the work I had done during the day. All of a sudden I heard Mom call out: "Come on Keta, dinner." Needless to say, she didn't have to call me twice. As soon as I heard her call I turned on my afterburner and headed for the galley where I found my first freshly cooked salmon dinner waiting for me. I really made a real pig of myself and gulped it down as if I had not eaten in a week. It was so delicious and I knew then that I had made it to kitty heaven.

This is the story of how I became a Sea Cat. In all honesty I must admit it is going to be a great life. My only regret so far is that I have not yet been able to convince Dad to promote me to Captain. If and when that occurs, the story will be a real "Cat's Tale."

Respectfully, Keta, a cat named after a salmon named after a dog, living the good life on the F/V LaDonna Rose.

Coconut Macaroons

These sweet and chewy two-bite macaroons are absolutely irresistible!

MAKES ABOUT 40 MACAROONS

- 1 (14-ounce) bag shredded sweetened coconut
- 1 (14-ounce) can sweetened condensed milk
- 1 teaspoon vanilla extract
- 2 large egg whites
- ¼ teaspoon sea salt
- 4 ounces bittersweet chocolate, melted

Preheat your oven to 350 degrees.

Line two baking sheets with parchment paper. In a medium bowl, combine the coconut with the sweetened milk and vanilla. In another bowl, using an electric mixer, beat the egg whites with the salt until firm peaks form. Fold the beaten whites into the coconut mixture.

Using a tablespoon and your fingers, form macaroons into mounds about 1-inch apart. Bake until macaroons are golden about 20 minutes. Transfer baking sheets to a cooling rack and let cool completely.

Dip the bottoms of the macaroons into the melted chocolate, letting any excess drip back into the bowl. Return the cookies to the lined baking sheets. Drizzle any remaining chocolate on top and refrigerate for about 5 minutes, until set. Store in an airtight container for up to a week.

Recipe hint

To avoid puddling when baking, the cookies must be baked as soon as they are combined with the egg whites. If you wait too long the egg whites will break down and cause them to be runny and they will puddle. They are still delicious and my favorite part of the macaroon.

Rhubarb Crumble

This crumble is quick and easier to make than pie. It's versatile, too, because you can add strawberries in the spring or apples in the fall. I usually pop it into the oven shortly before we sit down to eat so it's still warm for dessert!

Preheat your oven to 350 degrees. Evenly coat an 8 x 8-inch baking dish with nonstick cooking spray.

MAKE THE TOPPING: In a food processor, combine the flour, brown sugar, oats, cinnamon and ¼ teaspoon salt and pulse several times to combine. Add the cold butter and pulse until the mixture has the texture of course meal and clumps together when squeezed lightly, about 1 minute.

MAKE THE FILLING: Combine the rhubarb, brown sugar, cornstarch, lemon juice, lemon zest and ¼ teaspoon salt in a large bowl and stir with a spatula until evenly mixed. Transfer the rhubarb mixture to the baking dish and sprinkle the topping evenly over the fruit; the pan will be very full, but the crumble will settle as it bakes.

Bake until the topping is lightly browned, the rhubarb is tender (probe in the center with a skewer to check) and the juices are thick and bubbly around the edges, 45-60 minutes. Transfer to a rack to cool and to allow the juices to thicken, at least 15 minutes.

SERVES 4

FOR THE TOPPING

- 1 cup all-purpose flour
- 1 cup lightly packed light brown sugar
- ½ cup old-fashioned oats
- ½ teaspoon ground cinnamon
- sea salt
- ½ cup (1 stick) cold butter, cut into small pieces

FOR THE FILLING

- 7 cups fresh rhubarb (about 2 lb.) ⅓ inch-thick sliced
- 1 cup lightly packed light brown sugar
- ¼ cup cornstarch
- 1 tablespoon lemon juice
- 2 teaspoons grated lemon zest
- sea salt

Recipe hint

If using frozen rhubarb, I would just make sure the rhubarb was well defrosted and drained first.

Mystery Bars

I have made a lot of bar cookies in my life, but these are definitely the best. Don't be surprised if someone asks you for the recipe!

MAKES ABOUT 2 DOZEN PIECES

40-50 saltine crackers
1 cup (2 sticks) butter
1 cup lightly packed light brown
   sugar
2 cups semi-sweet chocolate
   chips
1 cup walnuts, chopped

Preheat your oven to 350 degrees. Line a rimmed baking sheet with parchment paper. Place the saltine crackers in a row on the baking sheet, without any gaps.

Combine the butter and brown sugar in a saucepan and cook over medium heat until the mixture comes to a boil. Stirring constantly, boil for 3 minutes.

Spread the mixture over the crackers to cover completely. Bake until the caramel is bubbling, about 3 minutes.

Remove the baking sheet from the oven and quickly sprinkle with the chocolate chips, let them melt a bit and spread evenly around. Sprinkle nuts over the top.

Allow them to cool in the refrigerator for a few minutes before breaking apart into pieces.

Variation

Add or substitute peanut butter chips.

Cookie Brittle

Attention: This cookie brittle is straight up addictive. It will call you from the counter top all day long and when you go out, you'll think about it on your way home and feel the need to eat a piece before you even remove your coat. This is that sort of thing. You have been warned.

Preheat your oven to 350 degrees. Line a baking sheet with parchment paper.

Using a hand or stand mixer, cream the butter, sugar, salt and almond extract together on medium-high speed until nice and fluffy. Reduce the mixer speed to medium-low and add the flour. When the dough has absorbed the dry ingredients, stir in nuts and chocolate chips and mix until they are well distributed.

With your fingers, press dough onto the baking sheet. Dough will completely fill the pan but won't spread. Bake for 15-20 minutes or until the edges are nice and golden. Remove the baking sheet from the oven and allow to cool for 30 minutes. Then break apart.

MAKES ABOUT 2 DOZEN PIECES

- 1 cup (2 sticks) butter, softened
- 1 cup granulated sugar
- 1 teaspoon sea salt
- 1½ teaspoons almond or vanilla extract
- 2 cups all-purpose flour
- 1 cup sliced almonds
- 1 cup semi-sweet chocolate chips

Recipe hint

Make sure you press the dough as thin as you can-the thinner it is the more glorious it will be. Pop it into the oven and bake until it's a golden color. Now comes the hard part... waiting until it is totally cool before you break it up into brittle pieces. Lift up the mass and start breaking it up into whatever size pieces you like. After which you can give it away, keep it for yourself or split the difference.

Cookie Brittle

Key Lime Mousse in Gingersnap Bowls

Don't let the fancy name scare you—gingersnap bowls are easy to make. Filled with this refreshing mousse, it's the perfect dessert!

SERVES 4-6

FOR THE MOUSSE

½ cup (1 stick) butter

6 egg yolks
2 whole eggs
1 cup Key lime juice
¾ cup granulated sugar

1½ cups heavy cream
2 tablespoons confectioners'
    sugar
zest of one lime, minced, optional

FOR THE GINGERSNAP BOWLS

¼ cup all-purpose flour
¼ teaspoon ground ginger
3 tablespoons butter
3 tablespoons granulated sugar
2 tablespoons corn syrup
nonstick cooking spray

whipped cream, for serving
    (optional)

Recipe hint

Gingersnap bowls aren't hard to make, but they require careful timing and patience. Now I won't lie – I broke a few getting started, so if it happens to you, don't get frustrated. Trust me, the process gets easier as you go!

MAKE THE MOUSSE: In a heat proof bowl set over a pan of gently simmering water, melt the butter. Add yolks, whole eggs, juice and sugar. Cook over medium-high heat, stirring occasionally, until thick, about 10 minutes. Transfer to a bowl, cover with plastic wrap, (pressing over the surface) and chill until cold, about 1 hour.

Using a hand or stand mixer, beat the cream and sugar until stiff peaks form. Fold cream, cold curd and zest together in a large bowl. Cover and chill until set, at least 1 hour or overnight.

MAKE THE GINGERSNAP BOWLS: **Preheat your oven** to 350 degrees, with rack in center. In a bowl, whisk together flour and ginger. Melt butter in a saucepan over medium. Add sugar and syrup, cook over low, stirring with a wooden spoon, until sugar dissolves, 5-8 minutes. Remove from heat, stir in flour mixture. Cool completely, about 25 minutes.

Coat a baking sheet with cooking spray. Making two cookies at time, drop batter by level tablespoons onto sheet, at least 6 inches apart. Bake until batter spreads and is golden in center, 9-11 minutes (cooking times will be shorter for later batches). Coat baking sheet with more cooking spray before each batch. Let cool 30-40 seconds. Working quickly with a wide metal spatula, slide cookies onto two over-turned cups; mold with your fingers. Cool completely; remove from cups. Store in airtight container up to a week. To serve, fill bowls with mousse and top with whipped cream.

FOR THE CARDAMOM COOKIES

1½ cups (3 sticks) butter, softened
¾ cup granulated sugar
2 teaspoons finely grated orange zest
2½ cups all-purpose flour
1½ teaspoons ground cardamom
½ teaspoon sea salt

FOR THE FOOL

2 cups fresh raspberries
½ cup granulated sugar
1 teaspoon orange liqueur, optional
1 cup heavy cream
2 tablespoons confectioners' sugar
½ teaspoon vanilla extract

Variation Feel free to substitute black-berries, salmonberries, strawberries or blueberries.

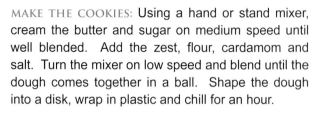

MAKE THE COOKIES: Using a hand or stand mixer, cream the butter and sugar on medium speed until well blended. Add the zest, flour, cardamom and salt. Turn the mixer on low speed and blend until the dough comes together in a ball. Shape the dough into a disk, wrap in plastic and chill for an hour.

Preheat your oven to 350 degrees. Line a baking sheet with parchment paper. On a lightly floured surface, roll the dough to a thickness of about ½ inch. Use a 2-inch cookie cutter to cut out circles of dough. Place the cookies on baking sheets with about ½ inch between the cookies. Bake on the center rack of the oven until the cookies are lightly browned, 12-15 minutes. Let the cookies cool before removing from pan. Serve with Raspberry Fool.

MAKE THE FOOL: Set a medium-mesh sieve over a medium bowl. Use the back of a wooden spoon to push 1 cup of the raspberries through the sieve, smearing the berries back and forth across the mash until only seeds and pulp remain. Scraping any purée from the bottom of the sieve. Stir in the sugar and orange liqueur into the purée.

In a medium metal bowl, combine the cream, confectioners' sugar and vanilla and beat with an electric hand mixer on high speed until soft peaks form, about 2 minutes.

Pour the raspberry mixture over the cream. Use a butter knife to gently stir the mixture so that thin streaks of raspberry juice runs through the cream. Spoon the mixture into four glasses or small dessert bowls and top with the remaining raspberries.

Raspberry Fool with Cardamom Cookies

This Raspberry Fool turns tangy raspberries and luscious whipped cream into a simple yet elegant dessert in a snap. Fold fresh raspberries—either lightly mashed or fully puréed—into a good quality whipped cream for a light, fluffy dessert that will wow your guests (and leave them disbelieving the dessert's simplicity). The liqueur is optional, but note that orange liqueur adds a lovely sweet citrus note that deepens the rich, berry flavor of this fool.

Flourless Chocolate Cake

This cake is the absolute definition of indulgence. It's the perfect lush decadence that only a truly great chocolate creation can provide. It's also the perfect way to end a romantic dinner.

MAKE THE CAKE: **Preheat your oven** to 350 degrees. Butter a 9-inch springform pan. Line the bottom of pan with parchment paper. Wrap outside of pan with foil. In a heat-proof bowl set over a pan of gently simmering water, melt butter and chocolate together. Stir until combined. Set aside to cool.

Using electric mixer, beat egg yolks and 6 tablespoons sugar in a large bowl until mixture is thick and pale. Fold melted chocolate into yolk mixture, then fold in vanilla extract. Using clean dry beaters, beat egg whites in another large bowl until soft peaks form. Gradually add 6 tablespoons sugar, beating until medium-firm peaks form. Fold egg whites into chocolate mixture in 3 additions. Pour batter into prepared pan.

Bake cake until top is puffed and cracked and tester inserted into the center comes out with some moist crumbs attached, about 45 minutes. Transfer cake to a wire rack to cool in pan, about 30 minutes.

Gently press down crusty top to make evenly thick cake. Using a small knife, cut around pan sides to loosen cake. Remove pan sides. Place 9-inch diameter tart pan bottom or cardboard round atop cake. Invert cake onto tart pan bottom. Peel off parchment paper.

Place cake on a rack set over a baking sheet lined with parchment paper. Spread ½ cup glaze smoothly over top and sides of cake. Freeze until almost set, about 5 minutes. Pour remaining glaze over cake; smooth sides and top. Place cake on platter. Chill until the glaze is firm. Garnish with whipped cream and fresh berries, if desired.

MAKES 8-10 SERVINGS

FOR THE CAKE

12 ounces bittersweet or semi sweet chocolate, chopped

¾ cup (1½ sticks) unsalted butter, cut into pieces, plus more for buttering the pan

6 large eggs, separated

12 tablespoons granulated sugar divided in half

2 teaspoons vanilla extract

FOR THE GLAZE

½ cup whipping cream

½ cup corn syrup

8 ounces bittersweet or semisweet chocolate, finely chopped

MAKE THE GLAZE: Bring cream and corn syrup to a simmer in medium saucepan. Remove from heat. Add chocolate and whisk until melted smooth.

Whipping Cream

For 2 cups sweetened whipped cream, you'll need **1 cup heavy cream, 2 tablespoons granulated sugar and 1 teaspoon vanilla extract.** Using a hand mixer begin beating on medium-high speed. Beat until desired consistency, about 2 minutes.

FOR THE GALETTE DOUGH

- 3 tablespoons sour cream
- 1/3 cup cold water
- 1 cup all-purpose flour
- 1/4 cup yellow cornmeal
- 1 teaspoon granulated sugar
- 1/2 teaspoon sea salt
- 7 tablespoons cold unsalted butter, cut into pats

FOR THE FILLING

- 3 to 4 apples, peeled, cored, halved and sliced crosswise into 1/4-inch-thick slices (about 3 cups)
- 2 tablespoons lemon juice
- 3 tablespoon light brown sugar
- 3 tablespoons maple syrup, divided
- 1 teaspoon ground cinnamon
- 3 tablespoons all-purpose flour, plus extra for rolling
- 1 tablespoon butter, diced

EGG WASH

- 1 egg yolk mixed with 1 teaspoon water
- 2 tablespoons raw sugar

MAKE THE DOUGH: Whisk the sour cream and cold water together in a small bowl, set aside. Mix the flour, cornmeal, sugar and salt in a bowl. Using a pastry blender, blend in butter until the mixture resembles small peas. Drizzle evenly with the sour cream mixture and gently stir until incorporated. Dough should be soft and moist. Remove the dough from the bowl and press into a disk. Wrap in plastic wrap and refrigerate for thirty minutes.

MAKE THE FILLING: Toss apples with the lemon juice, brown sugar, maple syrup, cinnamon and flour.

Preheat your oven to 400 degrees. Unwrap dough and place on a 16-inch piece of parchment paper that has been dusted with flour. Roll dough into a 14-inch circle. Place dough and parchment on a rimmed baking sheet, (dough will hang over the parchment) arrange apples in center, leaving a 2-inch border around the edges. Dot apples with butter. Fold the edges of the crust over the fruit, pleating the dough as you go and leaving the center exposed. Brush the outside edges with egg wash and sprinkle with raw sugar. Bake for 45 minutes or until crust is golden, filling is bubbly and apples are tender. Cut into wedges and serve.

Filling ideas

To be honest, you could pretty much use anything with a galette, as long as it's not too much liquid. Here are some ideas: plums, pears, peaches or nectarines.

Variations

Wow your dinner guests with simple, bite-size pastries. Serve each slice with a scoop of vanilla ice cream. Substitute one 9-inch unbaked pie crust.

Rustic Apple-Maple Galette

I love the simplicity of this dessert and it reminds me of home, warmth and love. It is so simple to prepare and never fails to impress friends and family.

Shut the Window Ole, I Have a Cake in the Oven!

One day while Ole and I were fishing, we began discussing stories we might include in our new book. We immediately agreed that one story we must include would be an explanation of how the little stove on our boat works and how it serves to not only heat the boat but also as the stove and oven I use to cook all our meals. When the time came to actually begin writing the story about our little stove, we were anchored in a quiet cove. We began brainstorming the things we could come up with on a note pad. Then, I began reading to Ole the various ideas we had written down and he would give each idea a thumb up or a thumb down. The following "tiny oven" story includes all of the things we agreed were deserving of being included in this book.

The first thing we do when we get on our boat is to light the oil stove to heat the cabin. Lighting our tiny oil stove is not as easy as you might think. First, the valve on the oil line that supplies oil to the stove must be turned on in order for oil to drip into the bottom of the stove's fire pot. Next, we must wait until just the right amount of oil is in the fire pot before it can be lit. If we become distracted during this time period and too much oil pools in the fire pot, the stove will become flooded and further action is needed before it can be lit. Once the proper amount of oil has pooled in the fire pot, one of us must light a small piece of paper towel and drop it into the stove so that it falls into the pot. If the burning paper towel falls off to the side, there will be no ignition and we must try again. Generally, we use a larger piece of paper towel if a second attempt is necessary and make certain it is burning fully before it is dropped into the stove. This can result in what Ole and I call a "Lighting Ouch," if we burn our fingers; and, even if we don't, the paper towel may extinguish before it ignites the pool of oil. If all else fails, we must resort to lighting an even larger piece of paper towel, dropping the burning towel into the stove and then using a piece of twisted wire Ole made specifically for this situation to push the burning towel into the pool of oil. Fortunately, Ole has mastered the lighting process well and when he lights the stove, he is successful at the first attempt.

As soon as the pool of oil has been ignited and begins to burn, we put the lid back onto the stove so the cabin does not fill with smoke and turn on the stove's circulating fan. Sometimes, to add insult to injury, after we finally get the pool of oil to begin burning, turning on the fan puts the fire out. This is what is known as a "real bummer."

Once the fire is finally burning properly, we watch it carefully and adjust it to the correct temperature. If the wind is blowing, we must adjust the windows; and, if we are underway, the front port and starboard windows must be closed and the back window and cabin door cracked. On one particular occasion, I had a cake in the oven and Ole was too warm so he opened the port window to cool off. I shouted "Shut the window Ole, I have a cake in the oven!" Unfortunately, before Ole could close the window, the wind blew in, created a vacuum in the fire pot, and put out the fire. The oil, which was still dripping, ignited the hot vapor gas which in turn blew off the lid of the stove. The end result was that my cake fell, smoke filled the cabin and little particles of black soot were everywhere. Our faces, hair and clothes were inundated with soot and we looked like a couple of coal miners who had just come out of the mine. We looked at each other and broke out laughing.

Luckily, this only happens once or twice each summer and always provides us with a good laugh.

Ole's Butter and Brown Sugar Squares

Let's just say they're utterly rich and sugary and if that's not enough, they're topped with a whiskey buttermilk butterscotch sauce. Yum!

MAKE THE SQUARES: **Preheat your oven** to 350 degrees. Butter a 9 x 13-inch baking dish.

Using a hand or stand mixer, cream the butter and sugars on medium-high speed for 2 minutes until nice and fluffy. Beat in the eggs one at a time, then add the vanilla, beating until smooth. Reduce the mixer speed to medium-low and add the flour, baking powder and salt. Stir in the pecans.

Pour the batter into the baking dish. Bake for 30 minutes or until tests done. Let the cake cool in its pan for 15 minutes. Cut into squares and serve with a spoonful of the sauce.

MAKE THE SAUCE: Combine sugar, buttermilk, butter and corn syrup in a small saucepan over medium heat. Cook, stirring constantly and simmer until the butter has melted and the mixture is smooth. Stir in the whiskey and nuts. Serve warm or at room temperature. Cover and keep refrigerated.

MAKES 16 SQUARES

FOR THE SQUARES

- 1 cup (2 sticks) butter, softened
- 2 cups firmly packed light brown sugar
- ½ cup granulated sugar
- 4 eggs
- 1 teaspoon vanilla extract
- 2 cups all-purpose flour
- 1 teaspoon baking powder
- ½ teaspoon sea salt
- 1 cup chopped pecans

FOR THE WHISKEY BUTTERMILK BUTTERSCOTCH SAUCE

- 1 cup granulated sugar
- ½ cup low-fat buttermilk
- ½ cup (1 stick) butter
- 2 tablespoons corn syrup
- 2 tablespoons whiskey
- 1 cup toasted chopped pecans, optional

whipped cream, for serving

Come on Over!

When you live in a remote environment that lends it's self to long days, hard work and at times extreme weather conditions, you will find Alaskans looking for any excuse to get together. Clear skies, warm sun and a day off is the perfect opportunity to gather with friends and family. The times that we get together we re-energize, regroup and celebrate the hard work that has been done and get ready for the work ahead.

Planning a party has its own rewards, when friends come tumbling in, good stories and laughter are not far behind. It's then you realize that you don't have to entertain. Happy people entertain themselves. It's enough to be together, having a good time. Of course, great food makes it even better!

Some occasions may call for extra planning, but are rewarded by the deep, lasting memories the moment creates. Those you love most around your table, back deck or campfire, these are the times we treasure.

In celebration of home, family and friends, we invite you to sample some of the best recipes and party menu ideas we have shared with each other throughout our Alaskan gatherings. Come on over and enjoy! ❧

Summer Kick Off

Assorted Beverages and Beer
Crab Croquettes
Pancetta Wrapper King Salmon Kebabs
Grilled Salmon Caesar Salad
Artichoke, Tomato and Spinach Pizza
Raspberry Fool with Cardamom Cookies

Seafood Extravaganza

Chilled White Wine
Crab, Shrimp and Pork Pot Stickers
Dungeness Crab Corn Chowder
Roasted Shrimp with Rosemary and Thyme
Seared Scallops with Teriyaki Salad
Bacon Wrapped Halibut
Raspberry Fool with Cardamom Cookies

Fourth of July Celebration

Assorted Beverages and Lemonade
Spicy Tomato Salsa with Tortilla Chips
Honey Mustard Coleslaw
Two Bean Rice Salad
Grilled Salmon with Cherry-Chipotle Glaze
Coffee Spice-Rubbed Spareribs
Rhubarb Crumble

Back Deck Party

Assorted Beverages
Perfect Guacamole
Dungeness Crab with Two Dipping Sauces
Coconut Shrimp with Green Goddess Dip
BLT Salad with Buttermilk Dressing
Three-Cheese Mini-Macs
Cookie Brittle

Outdoor Bonfire at the Beach

Warm Apple Cider
Chipotle and Rosemary Nuts
Crab Stuffed Mushrooms
Simple Stromboli
Mystery Bars

End of the Season Party

Assorted Beverages and Beer
Smoked Salmon with Wild Berries on Grit Cakes
Buffalo Chicken Wings
Soy-Glazed Black Cod with Orange Zest
Garlic-Coconut Sockeye Salmon
Perfect Rice
Apple Spinach Salad
Ole's Butter and Brown Sugar Squares

Birthday Celebration

Bordeaux or Riesling
Pan Fried Oysters with Tarter Sauce
Crispy Salad Stack with Orange-
Soy Vinaigrette
Pan-Roasted Rib Eyes
Roasted Cauliflower
Flourless Chocolate Cake

Romantic Dinner for Two

Pinot Noir or Zinfandal wine
Steamed Clams with Spicy Sausage and Garlic
Proscuitto Wrapped Nectarine Bites
Grilled Lamb Chops with Blueberry-
Rosemary Sauce
Caramelized-Onion Mashed Potatoes
Lemon Broccolini
Cream Puffs with Coffee Ice cream

The Morning After

Bloody Marys and Coffee
Currant Scones

Breakfast with Friends

Coffee and Mimosas
Sweet-and-Spicy Bacon
Apple Puffed Pancake

New Years Eve

Champagne or Sparkling Spumante
Bacon Wrapped Dates
Garlic Shrimp Crostini
Cheese Straws
Crab Salad on Corn Blini
Sesame Rice Cakes
Rosemary and Garlic Roasted Salmon
Key Lime Mousse in Gingersnap Bowls

Wine selection... made simple

Choosing the right wine to go with different kinds of food can be intimidating, but it doesn't have to be. Most importantly, select a wine that you enjoy, rather than following a set of rules. Never mind the old adage about white wines going with fish and red wines going with meat. In general, it's good to choose a lighter wine, whether red or white, for lighter foods or to enjoy alone and choose heavier and more full-bodied wines for heartier and richer foods.

The following guide may help you in your choices. These are suggestions of types of wine, not brand names. Also, be aware that any guide like this is open to interpretation and question. If possible, find a local wine store with a good reputation where the staff can help you further define wines that suit your taste and budget.

Alone or with Appetizers

Red — Beaujolais, Pinot Noir, Sangiovese

White — Sauvignon Blanc, Chablis, Riesling, Pinot Blanc, Champagne, Muscato, Spumante

Seafood

Red — Pinot Noir, Burgundy, Malbec, Merlot

White — Vouvray, Fumé Blanc, Sauvignon Blanc, Pinot Grigio, Chablis, Chardonnay, Viognier

Poultry

Red — Pinot Noir, Burgandy, Malbec, Merlot

White — Sauvignon Blanc, Fumé Blanc, Chardonnay, Riesling, Pinot Blanc, Gewürztraminer, Viognier

Beef

Red — Cabernet Sauvignon, Bordeaux, Pinot Noir, Burgandy, Petite Syrah, Merlot, Shiraz, Rioja

Lamb

Red — Pinot Noir, Bordeaux, Burgandy, Cabernet Sauvignon, Malbec, Merlot

Pork

Red — Pinot Noir, Burgandy, Beaujolais, Sangiovese

White — Johannisberg Riesling, Gewüztraminer

Salads

Red — Beaujolais, Sangiovese

White — Fumé Blanc, Sauvignon Blanc, Riesling

Cheese

Red — Cabernet Sauvignon, Bordeaux, Burgundy, Shiraz, Port

White — Riesling, Chardonnay, Champagne

Fruits

Red — Port

White — Riesling, Vouvray, Chenin Blanc, Gewürztraminer, Champagne

Desserts

Red — Port

White — Riesling, Champagne, Moscato Spumante, Prosecco

Cook's Notes

One of my favorite things has always been cooking and I thought I'd go nuts on board with my normal style, so I have adjusted to a more relaxed style – Less things on the plate, higher quality ingredients (when available) and great flavors. We eat as healthy as possible and most always from scratch. With basic ingredients on board, you can make anything you want and with a couple of cookbooks that use everyday ingredients, can really give you a lot of confidence.

Cooking smarter to get meals on the table quickly, I've learned a few time saving tricks.

1. GET A HEAD START Read the recipe from beginning to end, then measure, prep and place ingredients in bowls or on the cheapest paper plates, (great for small space cooking and clean up) so everything's at the ready as you cook.

2. KEEP YOUR COOL Buy meat and poultry in bulk and freeze in individual portions for faster thawing. Freeze pesto and tomato sauce too, for a last-minute pasta toss.

3. STOCK THE PANTRY Keep shelf-stable meal-building staples on hand. I like canned beans, tomatoes, artichokes, chicken, salmon as well as organic box chicken and vegetable broth, along with pasta and rice. Basics such as oils, vinegars, mustard, mayonnaise, soy sauce, pickle relish and powdered buttermilk are always useful.

4. FLAVOR IN A FLASH Store a big batch of your favorite spice rub to season chicken, pork or fish before roasting.

5. THINK DOUBLE DUTY Make extra vinaigrette to marinate meats. Or stir olive oil into salsa and use it as a sauce for chicken or fish.

6. USE PARCHMENT PAPER A huge helper with baking and cooking, you'll never have to worry about cookies or fish sticking to your pans. Using parchment paper makes life a bit less stressful.

7. INVEST IN TIME-SAVING KITCHEN TOOLS A mini food processor, a quality chef's knife, an electric hand mixer and flexible chopping mats, truly makes life a bit easier.

Yes, there are many challenges cooking in a Rock'n Galley with a Tiny Oven, but without the challenges there is no adventure. It's really not all that bad once you get the hang of it.

Useful Conversions

Oven Temperatures

275°F = 135°C = gas mark 1
300°F = 149°C = gas mark 2
325°F = 163°C = gas mark 3
350°F = 177°C = gas mark 4
375°F = 191°C = gas mark 5
400°F = 204°C = gas mark 6
425°F = 218°C = gas mark 7
450°F = 232°C = gas mark 8
475°F = 246°C = gas mark 9

Dry Measures

1 cup	= 8 fluid ounces	= 16 tablespoons	= 48 teaspoons
¾ cup	= 6 fluid ounces	= 12 tablespoons	= 36 teaspoons
⅔ cup	= 5 fluid ounces	= 10⅔ tablespoons	= 32 teaspoons
½ cup	= 4 fluid ounces	= 8 tablespoons	= 24 teaspoons
⅓ cup	= 2⅔ fluid ounces	= 5⅓ tablespoons	= 16 teaspoons
¼ cup	= 2 fluid ounces	= 4 tablespoons	= 12 teaspoons
⅛ cup	= 1 fluid ounces	= 2 tablespoons	= 6 teaspoons
		1 tablespoon	= 3 teaspoons

Liquid Measures

1 gallon	= 4 quarts	= 8 pints	= 16 cups	= 128 fluid ounces
½ gallon	= 2 quarts	= 4 pints	= 8 cups	= 64 fluid ounces
¼ gallon	= 1 quart	= 2 pints	= 4 cups	= 32 fluid ounces
	½ quart	= 1 pint	= 2 cups	= 16 fluid ounces
	¼ quart	= ½ pint	= 1 cup	= 8 fluid ounces

INDEX

Acknowledgements

To my friends and family on and off land too numerous to mention, if you know me, you know who you are, thank you for loving me enough to encourage me to write this cookbook. I appreciate you all so very much.

Everyone should have cheerleaders as encouraging as my mother and father in-law Eric and Kay Gundersen. I grew into a strong self reliant woman thanks to them encouraging me every step of the way, throughout my married life. Without their unending love and support, I would not be where I am now.

To our forever friends Sande and Mary Tomlinson, sharing our time together in Florence, Oregon is amazingly fun. Sande, I can not thank you enough for editing the stories in this book.

Thank you Deby Santos, Michael Briggs, Marc Osborne, Gale Skaugstad and Howie Cusack, your enthusiasm and vision have made the cover something special.

Thank you Laurel Lyndal for going beyond the extra mile for me and writing the **Where Women Cook** article. You inspire me to keep moving forward.

To our Maui friends Brad Salter and Lida Zwi, we are eternally grateful for teaching us the true spirit of Aloha.

Thank you Ken and Lynora Eichner for helping me out in a cooking bind.

Thank you Ellie Duree for your friendship and all your help while we are away at sea.

To Carissa Peltier at Above and Beyond Salon. Thank you for making me look and feel like a million bucks before and after a long hard fishing season.

To Steve and crew at Green Coffee Bean and Shannon and crew at Dutch Bros. Thank you for keeping us going during the writing of this book.

Vered Mares who edited and packaged this book before sending it off to the printer. Thank you!

And to my husband, for being my best friend, daily taste tester, dish washer, photographer, co-author and the love of my life. Every aspect of writing this book with you has been a wonderful incredible journey.

Photography Credits:

A million thanks to the the following people for helping us out so we could do this book. *Page 12:* us holding fish, photo by Michael Harrell. *Page 13 and 39:* us unloading salmon, photo by Kenny Hamilton. *Page 45:* Classic Tours, Louis Munch. *Page 45:* us at the premier of Ketchikan a Fish Story, photo by Marc Osborne Jr. *Page 48:* City of Wrangell, photo by Carol Rushmore. *Page 90:* Sitka, photo by Dawn Johnson. *Page 108:* Whale Tale, photo by Susan Hoyt. *Page 138:* Juneau, courtesy of Juneau Convention & Visitors Bureau. *Page 160:* Haines Cannery, photo by Lori Stepansky. *Page 194:* Kiss and backdeck, photo by Daniel Badgley. *Page 195:* us at Hole in the Wall, photo by Michael Harrell. *Page 200:* Skagway, courtesy of Skagway Convention & Visitors Bureau. *Page 231:* us with fireworks, photo by Brad Salter. *Page 233:* Bon Fire, photo by Sarah Mastroyanis. *Page 244:* Our boat, photo by Janie Harrell. *Back Cover:* Kiss, photo by Daniel Badgley. ✤

The End